PENGUIN BOOKS

PROSPECTUS FOR A HABITABLE PLANET

Dan Smith is vice-chairperson of CND. E. P. Thompson is a vice-president of CND. They were both among the founders of END and in 1980 they co-edited the Penguin Special, *Protest and Survive*.

PROSPECTUS FOR A HABITABLE PLANET

EDITED BY DAN SMITH
AND E. P. THOMPSON

PENGUIN BOOKS

Penguin Books Ltd, Harmondsworth, Middlesex, England
Viking Penguin Inc., 40 West 23rd Street, New York, New York 10010, U.S.A.
Penguin Books Australia Ltd, Ringwood, Victoria, Australia
Penguin Books Canada Limited, 2801 John Street, Markham, Ontario, Canada L3R 1B4
Penguin Books (N.Z.) Ltd, 182–190 Wairau Road, Auckland 10, New Zealand

First published 1987

Made and printed in Great Britain by
Richard Clay Ltd, Bungay, Suffolk
Typeset in 10/12 pt Plantin

Contents

Preface

In 1980 we edited together the Penguin Special, *Protest and Survive*. That book became very widely accepted as a statement of the position of 'the peace movement', in Britain and beyond. We now return with two of the former contributors (Mary Kaldor and Bruce Kent) and with several new ones, to review old themes and to present new ones.

We have protested and we have survived. But non-stop protest becomes exhausting, and mere survival is a poor fruit for 'advanced' civilization to bear – a passing on of the present time's crisis unresolved to the next generation. The planet remains divided into two armed camps and the true business of civilization is to search for solutions which might bring this condition to an end. If this is not done, then it is possible that – at some moment in the twenty-first century – the planet will become uninhabitable. We offer a prospectus which could lead to an alternative future.

This book is as much concerned with political, diplomatic and economic structures and alternatives as it is with military. It analyses the sources of the continuing Cold War, and explores the possible alternatives of de-alignment in Europe, of non-provocative forms of defence, of a new plural diplomacy which relates the interests of the North and South. It envisages what a continent at peace might be like, and the role of private citizens and of peace movements in bringing this about. If we attend most closely to the problems of Europe, this is because that is where we live and work, and that is where our own contribution to the prospectus of global peace must, first of all, be made.

The views expressed by each contributor are her or his own. But contributors have met for discussions and have exchanged views with each other. When we came to envisaging what a continent at peace might be like we decided to move outside our own island perspectives and to invite guests from the continent to give us their own: Caesar Voûte from Holland, Jiri Dienstbier from Czechoslovakia, and Zdena Tomin (as she explains) from neither half of Europe and from both.

Too many people have helped us with advice or material for us to thank each one individually. We are glad to thank them collectively now. And acknowledgements are due to the *New Statesman*, in which a version of Zdena Tomin's essay first appeared, and to *Labour Focus on Eastern Europe* and to Mark Jackson, the translator, who first made available Jiri Dienstbier's essay.

August 1986

Dan Smith
E. P. Thompson

PART ONE

Analysis

1 E. P. Thompson: The Rituals of Enmity

In received wisdom the world's peace movements 'failed' between 1980 and 1984. The huge constituency in America supporting a freeze has given way to a populist majority endorsing President Reagan. *Protest and Survive* identified a central terrain of challenge as NATO 'modernization', and called for the refusal of Pershing II and cruise missiles. Despite massive protest movements this challenge failed and NATO's plans were put into effect. The Soviet military 'responded' in the same coin – as we had foretold they would – and introduced missiles into Czechoslovakia and East Germany.

That was a defeat, not just for the peace movement and its political allies, but for any prospect of a healing process between the blocs. And if we measure prospects of survival by counting weapons, we are surrounded by evidence of defeat. Not only are all the old obscene nuclear actors still in place, but nerve gas, the X-ray laser and all the exotic furniture of Star Wars are joining the cast. If we count weaponry, then the armourers have won.

This is not, fortunately, the only way of counting. Historians of protest movements know that they do not often attain their goals at their first moment of assertion. What they do, more often, is transform the climate of expectations and redefine the limits of what is politically possible (and impossible). The 'statesmen' then adjust their sails to the winds of opinion and steer new courses, looking out for a safe haven of compromise.

Since 1980 the climate of world opinion has changed in this way. In the Soviet Union, as a result of internal processes of change, a new leadership is showing more diplomatic flexibility. China appears to be lending its influence to the non-aligned world. In Western Europe the long reign of Atlanticist 'consensus' has been broken. NATO ideologues are holding their breath lest the West German and British elections should reverse the outcome of 1983. And the high theatre of Summit meetings and arms-control proposals is now played out in the face of an alert world audience. The aim of some of the participants may be less to control armaments than to control and pacify us, even if the cost of this may be – but only *in extremis* – some actual steps to disarm.

Seen from this aspect, the armourers might seem to be living on borrowed time. But that view is too optimistic. They are more cautious than they were and more attentive to public relations. Yet all the old arms agendas, as well as new ones, remain in place. What we are living through now, in political terms, is a stalemate, in which the armourers and the disarmers are blocking each others' moves.

The time has come for the forces of peace to take initiatives of new kinds to break this stalemate. Such initiatives need not necessarily be limited to disarmament proposals. There were times, between 1980 and 1984, when the peace movement's single-minded focus upon nuclear weaponry – and, indeed, upon particular nuclear weapons – became obsessional. The refusal of nuclear weapons is honourable and, in the perspective of civilization's survival, an ecological imperative. All the contributors to this book endorse this refusal. The rising world-wide anti-nuclear consciousness is a necessary precondition for any politics of peace. Yet it does not, in itself, prescribe such a politics. For the central condition out of which the nuclear weapons come is the bipolar confrontation of the Cold War, and this is expressed as much in political and ideological as in military forms. The three must be taken together. It is as necessary to rewrite the political and ideological texts of the Cold War as the military.

Moreover this presents us with opportunities. Confronted by weaponry we can say little more than 'no', or 'control', or 'disarm'. Small or middle-sized nations cannot do much about the arms race between the giants. They must wait around outside Summits or Geneva negotiations like a chorus, catching at the coat-tails of the superstars.

But in political or ideological matters their space for independent movement may be large, and, in the case of the United Kingdom, very much larger than decades of pliant Atlanticist self-submission has led us to suppose.

This planet's problem today may not be that the U S A and the U S S R insist upon keeping up a forty-year-old quarrel. It may be in the fact of the bipolar division of global power itself. Given this bipolar division, and the structuring of military power into the hands of two superpowers and their clients, it becomes inevitable that the two sides never *can* agree. They have become locked into a state of antagonism in which the least concession is blocked by nice calculations of advantage. Like wrestlers in combat, the hostile posture must be maintained with every nerve, since any weakening would lead to overthrow.

It may follow that the best hopes of survival lie in a return to plural or polycentric diplomacies, in which the lesser nations turn their backs upon the bipolar superpower theatre and start to take new initiatives among themselves. China is now urging this course, and there are premonitions that West European nations may follow. Strategies of de-alignment in the West will find a cautious echo among East and Central European nations, and will meet with a ready response from non-aligned forces in the Third World. As the audience begins to troop out of the bipolar theatre, so the superstars might begin to find it easier to come to a compromise with each other, in which the lesser nations act less as chorus than as mediators.

I will suggest at the end of this chapter some reasons why an unsuccessful middle-rated power, Britain, might, at this moment of stalemate between the armourers and disarmers, take an initiative which would call in question the whole rationale of the Cold War. But first I must offer an alternative reading of that Cold War, less in its recent military and political evolution (which is the theme of Dan Smith's chapter) than in its historically inherited form as rival armoured ideologies.

Anyone under the age of fifty grew up – or was born into – a world already glaciated into its Cold War form. It must seem to be like an immutable fact of geography that the continent of Europe is divided into two blocs which are struck into postures of 'deterrence' for evermore. Yet this 'fact' may yet appear to future historians as an abnormal and temporary state of affairs.

Independent of the causes and occasions of its origin, it is possible to see the Cold War as an inherited state of antagonism which has, in the course of several decades, found permanent structural and institutional expression. The adversary posture of the blocs continues not just because of habit or inertia – it is rooted in military and ideological forms which ensure that it is self-reproducing. The Cold War is not only a condition, it is also a *direction* towards which both blocs are being drawn, independently of the intentions of political leaders. These leaders are like driftwood carried onward by the current, who themselves have no notion of their destination.

The destination is terminal war and all the actors (including the drifting 'leaders') will be appalled when they reach it. They will reach it because, in the decades since the Cold War started, the rival blocs have been ceaselessly manufacturing the means and the mentalities of the Third World War. Even the world leaders agree, at summit meetings, that this is a risky state of affairs. But they privately resolve that it is safer to go on as they are than to try anything else. A little adjustment to the system here or there, perhaps – at the least, a new 'hot line', at the best a test ban treaty. But any true alternative might 'de-stabilize' what has become a familiar set of structured relations.

This is partly because, over the decades, a whole cluster of powerful interests have grown up which find the condition of permanent confrontation to be functional. And these interests are in a reciprocal relationship to matching interests on the other side, and continually excite each other to responses in the same kind. The armourers incite the other's armourers, the hawks feed the hawks, the ideologists rant at each other like rival auctioneers, and the missiles copulate with each other and breed on each others' foul bodies the next generation of missiles.

This relationship of reciprocity is not the same thing as 'symmetry'. I do not mean that Communism and Western capitalist democracies are converging into the same kind of social system. They remain distinct, with distinct histories and cultural traditions. So far from 'converging', the Cold War sets them on collision course, and makes impossible any healing process between them.

Yet the reciprocal antagonistic relationship with each other profoundly shapes the forms and directions of change on both sides: the allocation of resources and skills, the priorities of production and of technological research, the supreme imperatives of 'defence', the competition for clients, bases, resources and arms customers in every corner of the world. (This also structures and deforms all relations between the North and the South.) Hence, out of their two opposing social systems the opposed blocs have made something like a *third* system in which they are simultaneously antagonists and partners: the Cold War.

This third system determines the evolution of both, by imposing limits upon political possibilities and by imposing the priorities of militarism. And the habit of antagonism has become functional to interests on both sides. Clearly it is functional to very powerful specialist interest groups in the military, the research laboratories, the armourers and arms traders, the professionals in the intelligence and 'defence community' – in short to those interests combined together in what General Eisenhower described more than thirty years ago as the 'military–industrial complex'. This complex is immensely stronger than it was in Eisenhower's time, and in Washington it lobbies nakedly and incessantly, and was a major promoter of 'Star Wars'.

These interests cannot be sustained without the appropriation of huge resources from the public, in the form of taxes, deprivations and deferred expectations. Hence it is necessary to reproduce and keep refreshed popular fear of the enemy Other in order to legitimate these appropriations. In diplomacy the Cold War is eminently functional, to the point of cynicism; whatever a superpower wishes to do can be justified by fear of the Other. This is always the effective argument in exercising control over client states or 'allies'. It is also convenient as an apologia for quite old-fashioned acts of great-power intervention or aggression, in Asia, Central America, or Africa. Finally, the Cold War continues to serve, in different ways on each side, as a means for domestic social and political control.

No one planned or foresaw all this when the Cold War first glaciated between 1948 and 1951. Maybe we still underestimate the element of accident or contingency in the event. No doubt it was inevitable that there should be conflict when, at the end of the Second World War, the armies of the Soviet Union and the Western Allies met in Central Europe. But it was not inevitable that this conflict should become systemic and self-reproducing into future decades. It was the coincidence of the production of nuclear weapons at the very moment when these armies met which caused the 'Yalta' division of the continent to set in its condition of permafrost. The antagonism of the United States and the USSR was, paradoxically, like a magnetic force which held their forces in Europe, East and West, and prevented them from disengaging from each other.

In the years that followed, 'deterrence', or the 'balance' of nuclear threat, arrested all other kinds of political or diplomatic process. The ultimate nuclear threat imposed – and still imposes – a false 'stability', in which nuclear weapons serve to *suppress* the political resolution of differences. It may be argued – although this can never be proved – that they also suppressed the outbreak of conventional wars in Europe on the scale of those in Korea and Vietnam. But repression is not resolution. To 'deter' is also to defer, and to pass on each festering problem unresolved to future generations. Deterrence is the substitution of the threat of annihilation for negotiation.

Inevitably such a condition of repression backs up within both sides. The Cold War was also internalized. The high expectations for the deep democratization of political and economic life which flourished on both sides of the Atlantic at the end of the Second World War were disappointed. In America the era of the New Deal collapsed into McCarthyism. And while the American people have climbed out of that trough, and made gains in civil rights, the legacy of the first Cold War endures domestically as a pervasive resistance to any affirmative collective programmes (which are feared as 'communistic' or 'anti-American') and as a licence to every kind of exploitation of the public by private capitalist interests, especially the armourers.

In Western Europe this Cold War repression defeated the popular front alliances of 1945 – with the aid of the Marshall Plan – and isolated the Communist Parties as pariahs. In subsequent decades élites and Establishments which felt themselves to be threatened in 1945 have regrouped and regenerated themselves: the military, the security services, the sequestered higher civil service, the controllers of opinion. Money has broken loose from controls and privilege has thrown up new defences. Not all of this seedy evolution can be laid at the door of the Cold War. But at critical moments the imperatives of 'defence' and the media-induced panic about 'pro-Soviet' disloyalty or socialist 'extremism' have contributed to democracy's defeat.

Initially the consequences of Cold War repressive 'backup' were far more savage in the Communist bloc. The severe repression and mendacity of Stalin's last years still remain today the paradigm of 'Communist totalitarianism', and the traumatized memories of it are the only good argument on the side of the Western Cold Warriors. (Among other 'enemies', Stalin's terror fell with fury upon the 'revisionist' – democratic, humanist and nationalist – elements within the Communist Parties themselves: that is, those elements most likely to heal the broken blocs.) Since the high tide of late Stalinism this totalitarianism has been moderated: prison camps have shrunk in size, show trials and frame-ups have given way to bureaucratic invigilation, and the client states of Eastern and Central Europe have diversified in their economies and traditions. Yet each strong impulse of self-reform within the Communist bloc – Khrushchev's 'thaw', Nagy's bid for socialist humanism, the Prague Spring of 1968 and Polish Solidarity – have been contained and then repressed in the name of the imperatives of Communist Party control in the face of Western imperialism.

The onset of the 'new' Cold War reactivated all the traumas of the old one. The actual clash of interests which first occasioned the Cold War have been forgotten, but the old ideological scripts were dug out of the drawers and rehearsed as ideological farce. In this perspective the whole Euro-missile crisis of 1980 to 1983 can be seen in its full absurdity as an episode of classic Cold War 'functionalism' impelled far more by ideological bigotry than by any credible military rationale.

The intermediate nuclear missiles of both sides were never essential for reasons of 'defence'. Yes, in the ultimate worst case, they could – and may still be – used. But their immediate function is not military at all. They are symbols of 'posture' or 'messages'. As messages they are like great blasts of halitosis blown into the face of the Other.

As symbols they signified status and 'face', and the hegemony of each superpower over its own client states and its right to deposit its own nuclear excreta upon their territory at will. Even the ardent apologists for cruise and Pershing II missiles now confess (in the privacy of their expert journals) that the whole affair was a botch. The cruise missiles probably won't work (they keep flying off course on their tests to the terror of the bears and beavers in northern Canada). It was folly to put them down in little exposed cowpats dotted over Western Europe (Greenham, Comiso, Woensdrecht): the USA has far more cruise missiles coming along at sea and in the air which will be safer not only from enemy targeting but also from obstreperous women. Forcing the things down the throats of hostile publics gave the Establishment nightmares which it never wishes to go through again. No one can even remember now exactly why the damn things were ordered in the first place, except that they were in the armourers' catalogues, which the defence Establishment leafs through as excitedly as gardeners going through a catalogue of spring bulbs.

But once the things were ordered, ideology turned military rationality out of the driving-seat. In an infantile reversion to the worst-case hypotheses of 1948 we were told that only 'deterrence' prevented massed Soviet armour from rolling on Calais. As the opposition of the peace movement rose in Western Europe – and then in the USA – the drama became internalized. The Soviet SS-20s ceased to be the object of the exercise. The real object became to defeat the internal opposition. The American leaders needed to assert their domination over NATO clients and to hammer down their own objectors. The pliant European leaders who had learned by rote the dogmas of Atlanticism in their political cradles needed to affirm 'the unity and resolve of NATO'. They also needed to administer a punishing defeat upon their domestic opposition. Political life fell apart into a traditional left–right cleavage, and the right used every resource to isolate the opposition as 'pro-Soviet', defeatist and disloyal. By the time that cruise and Pershing II arrived it was clear that they were being pointed, as symbols, not at the Russians, but at the Greenham women, the Dutch Interchurch Peace Council, the Labour Party, the German Greens and CND. It was an exercise of domestic ideological and political control.

As for the Soviet leaders in the time of Brezhnev, Chernenko and Andropov, it is doubtful how far they believed their own propaganda that SS-20s were essential for 'defence' and that NATO modernization would bring Europe to the brink of nuclear war. Mr Gorbachov's agreement in Reykjavik to the withdrawal of all intermediate missiles from both sides of Europe might appear to come close to President Reagan's 'zero option', which Soviet leaders at that time denounced as a scandalous con-trick. This confirms that there never was any overwhelming military rationale for planting the SS-20s there in the first place: they were simply ordered because they were in the catalogue of spring bulbs.

It seems probable to me that the Soviet leadership of that time was astounded at the diplomatic bonus provided by the sudden emergence of a mass peace movement in the West, which (despite media fairy-tales) arose from non-aligned sources and quite independently of their manipulation. Initially they hoped to stand by and watch NATO screw itself up. By the summer of 1981 they were distracted by a quite different question – the breakaway triumphs of Solidarnosc in Poland and the threat which this offered to the discipline of the Warsaw Pact. When martial law was declared in Poland it marked another reversion to the norms of the 'old' Cold War, and the Cold War (and the Euro-missile crisis) became internalized within the Communist bloc also.

At that point the possible 'convergence' between elements in the Western peace movement and elements in the human-rights movement of the East came to be seen by Communist security organs as a major threat. We were aware, in the non-aligned peace movements, of a sudden hardening of Communist postures from the first months of 1982; the arrest or expulsion of Western peace visitors, the harassment of the Swords into Ploughshares young people in the GDR and of the Hungarian Dialog group, and zealous (but largely in-effectual) attempts of the old-style Soviet-controlled World Peace Council to meddle in the affairs of Western peace movements.[1]

This hardening was matched by a hardening of Soviet diplomacy during the slack tide of power between Brezhnev's death and Andropov's long last illness. The insecure Soviet leadership fell back into the old Cold War routines to which Gromyko was habituated. The threat of cruise and Pershing was used to rally their own public, to discipline their client states, to silence voices of dissent and to bring back Poland into subjection. It was also used to marshal such pro-Soviet forces as survive in the West, and as an apologia for building up SS-20 launchers. The SS-20s and then the SS-21 and SS-23s (planted symbolically as excreta on the territory of client states) became symbols, also, of 'the unity and resolve of the Warsaw Pact'. They were pointed, not at the West, but at Solidarnosc, Charter 77 and at any movement towards East European autonomy.

The whole episode, in retrospect, looks as meaningful as a Pavlovian reflex. Nothing was gained by either side, except greater insecurity. The most serious consequence was not this but the reactivation within the political cultures of both sides of old Cold War syndromes. In the Communist bloc voices and movements for human rights are again repressed as 'pro-Western', potentially treasonable and de-stabilizing. In the NATO bloc peace movements and their allies are again lampooned as 'pro-Soviet', potentially treasonable and de-stabilizing. On both sides the imperative of 'defence' has gained renewed authority as the supreme priority of state.

It is a commonplace that in times of war civil liberties are curtailed and emergency measures are rushed through, and that powers once granted in an emergency are not easily repealed. What distinguishes the Cold War era is that it has become possible to build the hypothesis of 'emergency' into the daily routines of the peacetime state. We do not confront any actual enemy; we have suffered no annexations, been issued with no ultimatums, our rulers confer with theirs and our traders trade. What we confront is an hypothesis: in some worst case the Other *might* be an enemy, or would be an enemy if it were not for nuclear 'deterrence'. The animating spirit of modern statism – a spirit which works in differing ways but with virulence on both sides of the Great Divide – is that of the permanent enemy hypothesis.

In Britain there has been for several decades a degenerative process at work, sapping the primary defences of the citizen against the over-mighty organs of the state. These primary defences were built up by piecemeal precedents over centuries, and they preceded and prepared the way for the full establishment of parliamentary democracy. They included such forms as habeas corpus, the integrity and rights of the jury, the subordination of military or police to the authority of the mayor, magistrates or civil power, the notional independence of the judiciary, the self-government of cities and corporations, the supposed (but only supposed) inviolability of the citizen's home and post (and by extension the telephone), and a culture which abhorred (even if it could not prevent) the planting of spies and informers in public societies.

More damage has been inflicted on this structure of primary defences in the past two or three decades than at any time since the Napoleonic Wars, if we except emergency regulations at the height of the First and Second World Wars. The Official Secrets Acts choke the corridors of power with evasion and mendacity. Excuses of 'security' remove the operation of the intelligence services from the scrutiny of the courts or of Parliament and threaten the press with prosecution. It was stated by a former security officer (Cathy Massiter) that CND and trade union phones were tapped and that agents have been planted in their offices, but this provoked no scandal and the judiciary forbade any inquiry. Mr Heseltine, when Secretary for Defence, set up from public revenue a partisan office in Whitehall (D S 19) whose function was to disseminate disinformation about the peace movement, and well before the next general election this unconstitutional office will be at work again. It has been revealed that for decades the staff of the BBC in sensitive, opinion-forming areas have passed through the screen of positive vetting. The police (and the Special Branch) are removed from civil control, juries are vetted in politically sensitive cases, trade union rights can be suspended (as at GCHQ Cheltenham), while security restrictions (sometimes with American oversight) extend to defence-related sectors of computer and high-tech industry and the CoCom regulations prohibit aspects of trade not only with Communist states but with neutrals such as Sweden, India or Ireland.

British society – like French or Dutch or Italian – now has a less active democratic temper, and feels less open to democratic renewal than it did in 1945. As central authority encroaches on old rights and assumes new powers – vets juries and abolishes the defence's right of challenge, dismisses elected local authorities, meddles with universities, assigns new powers and new weapons to the police, gets away with bugging our phones and planting agents in our offices – people lose confidence in their most ancient traditions. They lose the nerve of outrage.

The Cold War did not do all this. Terrorism has been a factor, the misery and racial tensions of the deprived inner cities another, and the 'liberation' of money to exploit us more nakedly has been another. But again and again some episode in the Cold War has reactivated the permanent enemy hypothesis, which has served as a legitimation to the most authoritarian forces in our society to enlarge their powers.

There are, of course, countervailing forces: this is not some closed authoritarian structure. Even vetted juries have refused to convict in 'sensitive' cases, and two civil servants who defied their political masters in the name of responsibility to truth and to Parliament, Sarah Tisdall and Clive Ponting, won the applause of a very substantial part of the public. The peace movement must be, in the West as well as in the East, a movement which defends all civil rights; for the cleansing and renewal of our democratic life is directly linked to the work of making peace.

In the Communist bloc, where official secrecy on 'defence' and many other matters is total, nevertheless one can see that (in much more difficult circumstances) a similar contest is going on. In Poland public outrage forced the trial and punishment of security police implicated in the murder of Father Jerzy Popieluszko – a trial without precedent in a Communist state. Human-rights campaigners or independent-minded peaceniks who have been persecuted for such 'sensitive' matters as communicating with the Western peace movement (for example, Ladislav Lis of Charter 77 in Czechoslovakia or members of the Moscow Group for Trust) have at least gone through the forms of trial. In the 1930s or in 1951 they would simply have 'disappeared'.

To notice this is not to condone the trials – nor the abuses of the psychiatric confinement of 'dissidents' and the daily harassment of unofficial peaceniks. It is to notice two important facts: first, there is a growing contest between an emergent civil society and the organs of state, in which Stalinist totalitarianism has been a good deal moderated by bureaucratic legal 'norms' and by a pressure of public opinion for more toleration; and, second, that the reciprocal relationship between the blocs does not always nourish the worst. It is not only the hawks who feed the Other's hawks. The doves may also take heart from each other's doves. Undoubtedly the Western peace movement has evoked responses in the East, and has even helped to open up some new spaces. Difficult as it is, through the jamming of the security services and the background blare of the ideological bands, independent voices on each side are beginning to talk to each other. We should never forget that the voices on the other side are putting themselves at risk.

I have suggested ways in which the Cold War may be viewed as a structured set of relations, which has become functional for certain interests and ruling groups on both sides. They do not 'want' nuclear war but they do need the Cold War to continue and would not know how to govern their halves of the world without it. Functionalism is, quite properly, disreputable among social thinkers today, so I must make it clear that I am indicating tendencies – the rules of the Cold War 'game' and the roles of the chief players – and not a closed and determined system.

The most pessimistic reflection upon this is that this 'game' is not a new one at all, it is as old as recorded history: only the enhanced means of destruction are new. As Sir Michael Howard has observed, 'self-identification as a nation implies almost by definition alienation from other communities'.[2] The very notion of nationhood is impossible without drawing boundaries between 'our' nationals and 'theirs'.

Every nation needs the idea of an Other (or others) to bind itself together in its own identity, and to that degree the

Other is a projection of its own need. And nations need the Other most of all when their own identity is blurred or insecure or when the rulers fear internal disaffection. Of course, if the Other presents itself as an actual enemy, then internal bonding against it becomes strong and the problems of the rulers are solved. The question, then, is: must the Other perforce be the Enemy? Is humankind doomed because the very same social mechanics which bond them together in nations require an enemy to bond against?

This is *the* question at the close of the twentieth century, and – while a hundred nationalisms now appear to grow in rancour – it is a question to be posed with especial urgency now to American and to Soviet reality. In the bipolar confrontation which now makes captive the globe, is there something other than conflicts of interest and the inertia of ideologies which perpetuates confrontation? Is there some special need for each superpower to have the Other as its Enemy today, for reasons of internal bonding and self-identity?

There are strong reasons to suppose that this could be so in the case of the Soviet Union, at least when it is viewed from outside its own ideological self-closure. A huge ramshackle quasi-empire, with many national and ethnic components, overripe for modernization and democratization, attempting to escape from the stultifying central controls of Stalinism and post-Stalinism, with an apathetic labour force, an economy overburdened by the efforts to match its military competitor, and with an increasingly restive periphery of unhappy allies – how can the rulers exert internal discipline and isolate 'dissident' elements, unless by gesticulating continually at the threat of the Western imperialist Other which menaces (as historical memories of earlier invasions confirms) the citizenry bonded together in the First and Foremost Socialist State?

Apart from any external attempts to 'de-stabilize' the regime – and such attempts are made – there are internal, self-generating forces making for 'de-stabilization'. If the physical and mental frontiers of the Soviet Union were to be, overnight, thrown open to the world, it is doubtful whether the social system could survive the apparent contrast between Soviet deprivation and Western 'affluence'. Hence even the cautious modernizers who are now attaining to influence within the Soviet Union may still require the Other. And President Reagan's USA, which has long been doing its best to look like a plausible threat and is now beginning to do its worst, is providing the necessary bonding which prevents the Communist bloc from undergoing any rapid diversification and change. It is not the Soviet people, but the Soviet military and the old post-Stalinist guard who need the Other very much.

But what about America? Here is another superstate, also too big for its own good, an ethnic miscellany assembled from the four corners of the globe. What provides bonding for this miscellany, what gives Americans their special self-image and sense of national identity?

There is much fine historical examination of American identity, but most of it is pursued introversially, from within. Was essential 'Americanism' the pursuit of freedom, opportunity and upward mobility; the newness of the New World; the frontier experience, the melting-pot, the tenacious coexistence of diverse ethnic traditions? Yes, it was something of all of those things. But what was *outside* the frontier? If these qualities contributed to Americanism, what was the *not*-American? What was the role of the Other in forming self-identity?

This question has not (to my knowledge) received the full investigation that it merits. An American scholar has noted that

> One of the many paradoxes of American history is how a nation of immigrants could be at the same time a nation that could so often be roused to fear and even hysteria over ideas, movements and people labelled as 'foreign' . . .[3]

This may be paradox: yet it may also be, precisely, the logic of bonding within a miscellaneous immigrant population, that there is an even greater need of the fear of Otherness to bond against.

The New World was also a world many of whose people were displaced persons. And to meet their insecurity unusual efforts (both consciously crafted and through less conscious forms of compensation) were made to construct an artificial identity of what it was to be 'American'. During the great immigrations from the 1850s to 1880s there was extraordinary selfconsciousness about indoctrinating the population (and the schoolchildren) with Americanism.

Moreover this self-image-making did not happen only once, it became obsessional within American culture. It went on and on and it continues today, in ways that seem to outsiders to be narcissistic, when commercialism and populist ideology conspire together to paint the whole sky with fireworks above the Statue of Liberty. Each year the culture puts on the production line a new model of the All-American Idea: a truly fearsome Disney-like confection, always young, sanitized, competitive, achievement-oriented, the utterly self-righteous guardian of every value known to time – conflict-free and completely characterless, with every wart removed, and in no way like the warty and incredibly various Americans whom we outsiders know, often admire, and have even been known to love.

As the late Warren Susman noted, 'the search for the "real" America could become a new kind of nationalism; the idea of an American Way could reinforce conformity'. It could, and does. But always in the pretence that it was not nationalism at all (of the Old World kind) – as indeed it was not – but was a denationalized universal: the Human Future. Identity required a sort of national superego, constructed more from ideology – the Idea of Americanism – than from history and contingency.

In her youth America had a palpable Other in our own reprobate nation, and for decades royal despotism and the Old World supplied the need for a foil, with the British still looming in Canada and the French and Spanish to the south. But the huge internal frontiers and the space of oceans protecting from invasion meant that the United States had less need for a foil than any other modern nation, and Americans could get on with making a genuine identity from their own resources and out of their experience of internal conflict and civil war.

A new phase commenced with the great immigrations of the second half of the nineteenth century. Now nativism, both élite and popular, identified all disorder with 'aliens' or 'imported beggars' and invaders. The *Chicago Times* regarded Slavic immigrants as descended from the Scythians: 'Let us ship these slavic wolves back to the European dens from which they issue, or in some way exterminate them.'[4] Employers identified the 'aliens' as 'socialists' (often German or Jewish) and, after the Haymarket affair in Chicago in 1886, as 'anarchists'. Ideas and values disturbing to dominant interests were thus identified as 'alien' and already – before the Second or Third Internationals were founded – the alien was taking on a red tinge.

'Alien' was to mark where the American frontier came to an end. This ideology grew, not in response to external armed threat, but out of the needs of internal discipline. The Other was not yet an Enemy Other of European type, fully fleshed out with the ethnic or racist chauvinism common to other nationalisms; although, as America's frontier extended into a world-wide dominion of interests and alliances, the palpable abrasion with others gave to it some of these tones.

Yet it remained possible, until well into the twentieth century, to suppose that Americanism was not a true nationalism at all. How could it be, when America encompassed all 'nations'? More than any other, American nationalism was an ideal construction, and Otherness was a projection of negative identity: what America was *not*, or what its dominant groups hoped it would not become. This found a late expression in isolationism, the refusal of the Other when the last post on the frontier had been reached. The frontier could be manned against aliens, and American nationalism could be self-sufficient, turning its back on Europe (although not on the Pacific or Latin America, where tacit imperial interests were given play).

Pearl Harbor destroyed that form of isolationism overnight, and the Second World War committed the United States deeply beyond its frontiers, taking over, among other burdens, many (Iran, Greece, the Middle East, Indo-China) which the weary white men of Europe had had to drop. But the confrontation of direct power interests with the Soviet Union and Communist China was decisive in giving to American nationalism a new (and, alas, all-too-recognizable) form. In one sense, some of America's rulers and employers had needed a Communist threat to bond their citizens against long before the Russian Revolution, and successive red scares had long prepared the channels. Now Soviet Communism and its agents took the whole role of negative identity, its totalitarian features providing a perfect identikit to match the part. This latest phase was signalled by the ritual execution of the Rosenbergs. When at length the Other could actually menace the American homeland with I C B Ms, the effect was traumatic, and when Sputnik bleeped innocently above the U S A the panic and outrage were comical: it was as if the American Dream had been violated.

At a time when other nationalisms were war-sick and growing weary, or were being a little moderated by the revolution in communications, America leapt into a new stage of nationalism. And the full assertion of American nationalism was the more brash and self-congratulatory in that it had been so long in waiting for its historical moment. In our own time – with a brief interval for Chinese Communism – Soviet Communism has fulfilled the needs for domestic bonding superbly, and has repaid in full measure the debt which the Soviet rulers owe to 'American imperialism' for performing the same function for them.

I place 'imperialism' in inverted commas, since I consider that the problem of America's aggressive postures in the world today stems from *nationalist* populist forces and ideological bombast, deliberately incited by interested parties, as much as from 'imperialism' (although there is also plenty of that). The approved self-image, the state-endorsed identity of an American national today is to be a Supernational of a state which arrogates to itself a divine right to go any place and bust in at any door in the name of its self-nominated leadership of 'the Free World'; which bombards and bombs around the shores of the Mediterranean without even consulting its NATO allies; which values American life in the scales several integers higher than any non-American mortalities; which rants about terrorism but nominates its own chosen terrorists in Nicaragua as 'freedom fighters'; which has fallen into many good old British habits in assuming a divine mission in the world; and which is locked in messianic combat with the Communist Other, whose ways and wiles are sufficiently defined when they are known as . . . un-American.

This sketch of the artificially confected Idea of American nationalism has been a brutal cartoon in child's crayons. I have lampooned the aggressive character of the Idea and said nothing of its domestic substance – the quite unusual assimilation of strangers and 'aliens' within American social life. I have said nothing of powerful alternative internationalist traditions, nor of alternative notations of what the American identity is or may be. Nevertheless I offer this cartoon because I believe that the dominant form of American nationalism is one of the most dangerous features of the world today. President Reagan is not some unfortunate political road accident, but the authentic communicator of this nationalist mood. It simply would not have been possible for America's leaders to have behaved in the world as they have done in recent years unless they had been supported by a profound populist constituency ever-ready to assume that America's mission must be 'moral', a 'manifest destiny' prescribed by God.

Maybe American rulers need Soviet Communism as the Other even more than the Soviet leaders need Western imperialism, and would need it whether it existed or not. I must watch my argument here with care. To say that the rulers need the threat of each other does not mean that there never has been and cannot be such a threat. On the contrary, the reciprocal need of both parties to project a hatred and fear upon each other, when this need is enforced not just by rhetoric but also by the very material contrivances of the respective military–industrial complexes, is exactly the way to exacerbate the threat and summon it into reality. It is a most menacing and self-confirming process, and it may be assuming ritual forms beyond the control of the actors. I am proposing that the ultimate cause leading to the Third World War is ideological, and that the ideological forces, and especially the nationalist drives, in both superpowers are in certain respects self-engendered and proceed from domestic needs.

The last six years have been very curious. The ideological motors of the Cold War have been whining to a crescendo, but most of all in the two superpowers which are most distant from each other. The allies and clients who lie in between – and who, one might suppose, stand in the immediate shadow of threat – have learned to lie snug a-bed o'nights. East and West Germans amicably exchange spies with each other, in rehearsed rituals, and then get around the table to explore new avenues of trade. Europeans, East and West, show signs of being more anxious at the gesticulations of their own guardian superpower than at the menace of the other. What alarms West Europeans most is the sense that the United States has become possessed with a new kind of supernationalism, very much like their own of yesteryear but more gargantuan in its self-esteem and appetites, whose very features are defined by anti-Communism: a nationalism which pretends that it is the universal human destiny.

It is not easy to know which frightens Europeans most. But in the past year or two, when a new generation of Soviet leaders have been slipping into power who have shown a quite new flexibility and who offer new spaces for genuine explorations in the making of peace, it is the mistiming of American truculence which alarms them most of all. When Mr Weinberger attends conferences of NATO ministers as if dressed up in combat fatigues and carrying an X-ray laser, like a messenger delivering a Rambogram, it is not only the peace movements which scoot for shelter. President Mitterand and Sir Geoffrey Howe dive under the nearest table and Chancellor Kohl is so nervous that he shoots himself in the foot.

The bipolarity of our world and the confiscation of the world's destiny into the control of the opposed superpowers is the greatest of our dangers. We need to rebuild a plural international community, with polycentric diplomacies, or the furious mutual incitements of bipolar Otherness will destroy us all. That is why we favour a strategy of detaching European nations, East and West, from either superpower pole, and forming good neighbourly relations with non-aligned nations in the Third World.

The objective would not be the formation of some third bloc, such as a West European mini-superpower. It would be to de-polarize the global antagonism and to interpose a mediating area between the over-mighty Others. It would initiate a healing process which could lead on to the dissolution (or gradual break up) of both NATO and the Warsaw Treaty Organization.

Such a strategy would be in the interests of the peoples of the superpowers themselves. Initially, the élites on both sides will resist it with every possible device, although its success may be the necessary precedent condition for them to come to some 'historic compromise' with each other. Such a compromise would signal the end of a whole era of Cold War. It would include, as one component, the agreed withdrawal of all Soviet and United States forces and bases from foreign territories. In Europe we might see the increasing 'Finlandization' of nations in East and Central Europe, and the 'Swedenization' of nations in the West.

This will not happen as a calm, controlled process; there will be sharp conflicts, untidy episodes, and fears of 'destabilization' along the way. The contributors to this book explore immediate and realistic policies which might advance this strategy. We may seem over-sanguine, yet we are heartened by the fact that the same hopes and similar strategies have arisen independently in many heads. Ideas precede effective political movements, and the sudden awakening of hopes that there might be an alternative to unending Cold War suggests that the time for these movements has now come.

It would, of course, be fruitless if these strategies were

only being discussed within the Western peace movement. But what is remarkable (although it has passed almost without remark in the major Western media) is that matching strategies are now under active debate in circles in the Communist bloc.

I refer to unofficial circles, since we can only guess at what discussions go on within the ruling bureaucracies. These unofficial circles are normally described in the West as 'dissidents', although they more often think of themselves as 'the constructive opposition' or as human-rights activists or as independent thinkers. In Western Cold War stereotypes it is supposed that there are only three possible political positions in the Communist bloc: the ruling CP apparatus, the cowed and apathetic majority, and a handful of courageous 'dissidents' who look to 'the Free West' for their eventual 'liberation'.

Western peace activists have travelled and communicated with the other side a good deal in the past few years, and we have found out that these stereotypes are fictions. Beneath the conformity imposed by the official media there is vigorous debate and a wide variety of opinions. It is clear that there are differences of view among the 'officials'. The level of international information is rising, in Moscow and Leningrad as well as in Warsaw and Prague. The younger generation share not only tastes in music but also ecological concerns (which have risen sharply after Chernobyl) and, with some modifications, feminist persuasions. As for human-rights activists, they were initially suspicious of the Western peace movement, which they supposed might be rigged and orchestrated by Soviet agencies. (Both their own and Western ideologues were anxious to convince them that this was so.) As communications improved, many of them have joined a transcontinental discussion as to how the causes of peace and of freedom might lend support to each other.

In a remarkable book, *Antipolitics*, the Hungarian novelist George Konrád wrote that

European identities are emerging at a critical pace in both East and

West. The mass movement against new missile deployment in Western Europe is more than just a protest against a concrete military measure ... It is a cry for autonomy, for the right of self-determination. We cannot allow the Soviet and American political élites to make the decisions that affect our lives. In both East and West, the European political vanguard has declared that our societies have the right to decide their own destinies ...

Although both superpowers regard it as the gravest offence for someone to 'drive a wedge' between them and their European allies, it seems to me that we Europeans can best safeguard the lives and security of Russians and Americans by extricating ourselves from their noisy quarrels ... The time has come to put compromise on the agenda – a historic compromise between the Soviet Union and the other European states, between the Russian people and the other peoples of Europe, between communists and non-communists.[5]

This is not a plea for East European states to change sides in the Cold War and enlist in NATO. It is a plea for states in both East and West Europe to detach themselves militarily from their superpowers 'and then go on to draw the two parts of a divided Europe together'. Konrád considers that 'if the population of Eastern Europe were to decide by referendum between neutrality or the Warsaw Pact, the majority would vote for neutrality'. Jiri Dienstbier considers that (if given a referendum) they would vote with overwhelming enthusiasm for 'the status of Finland' and would certainly prefer this 'to transferring their allegiance into the other camp'. People are sufficient realists to acknowledge that the Soviet Union has legitimate security interests on its Western glacis, and that good neighbourly relations with her are 'a basic necessity' (see p. 185).

The policies advocated by independent voices in the Communist bloc have many accents. Yuri and Olga Medvedkov and their friends in the Moscow Group for Trust have given most emphasis to enlarging direct citizen exchanges between the two sides. Sharper voices have come, especially from Polish KOS, demanding that the Western peace movement raises to first priority the ending of the

'Yalta' division of Europe. Mr Andras Hegedüs, who was once part of the Hungarian Communist hierarchy but who has maintained a stubborn critical independence ever since 1956, is more cautious. 'Ideological disarmament' and some measures of military disengagement must precede the re-unification of Europe: rather than 'pouring boiling water into a cold glass' we should 'simultaneously cool the water and warm the glass'.[6]

It is chastening to realize that some of the most searching transcontinental thought, and the most constructive strategies to bring the condition of Cold War to an end, have come not from the journals and research institutes of the 'Free West' but from people whose movements are under surveillance, whose meetings take place with difficulty, and whose statements may bring them within the shadow of prison. Such a man is Dr Jaroslav Šabata, who sent from Brno in 1983 a most searching letter to the Western peace movement, in which he invited us to confront together 'the all-important task of formulating a common, universal and all-embracing strategy for the democratic transformation of Europe', whose goal must be 'a democratic peace'. And he suggested a new concept of 'convergence', not of the two antagonistic social systems, but as 'the coming together of many initiatives, movements and the most varied forces . . . political, semi-political and "a-political" groupings', whose common demand must be 'to *abolish* the undemocratic legacy of the post-war social and political settlement, *end* the division of Europe into two opposing systems, and *unify* this artificially divided continent'.[7]

Dr Šabata is a member of Charter 77, and the fullest statement of this new perspective was issued, on 11 March 1985, in an Appeal from Prague over the signatures of forty-five Charter members. This called again for a strategy to overcome the division of Europe, 'a process of change [which] will call for great sensitivity. It cannot be accompanied by threats of achieving superiority on either side.' The signatories stressed the importance of the Helsinki agreement and the Helsinki process as a mechanism of change, not least because this process includes all states as equal partners and is not dominated by the superpowers. It criticized the Western peace movement for neglecting this process. It commended immediate measures such as disarmament initiatives, the creation of nuclear-free and neutral zones, and regional treaties, and raised the 'taboo' question of a German peace treaty, endorsing the right of the German people to self-determination. There should be no revision of European frontiers, but 'frontiers should gradually lose much of their significance':

> Another taboo subject has been the withdrawal of foreign troops. Let us therefore propose that N A T O and the Warsaw Pact enter forthwith into negotiations on the dissolution of their military organizations, on the removal of all nuclear weapons either sited in or aimed at Europe, and on the withdrawal of U S and Soviet troops from the territories of their European allies.

This should be accompanied by the scaling down of conventional armed forces. The letter was addressed to the forthcoming Convention of European peace movements (END) to be held that summer in Amsterdam.[8]

This historic Appeal provoked very little interest outside peace-movement circles. But it was not just some journalistic essay dashed off in an hour. It was a considered political statement, and we know that each line of it was scrutinized, debated and revised. Several signatories have at other times expressed criticism at silences or one-sidedness in the Western peace movement's activity; Vaclav Havel, the playwright, has asked why it has been so quiet about Afghanistan, and others have suspected it of giving lower priority to human rights than to peace. Yet these critics also gave their signatures to this positive platform for a democratic peace. Nor was it easy for them to do so. Some of their former colleagues, now expatriates in the West, accused them of complicity with 'Soviet-sponsored' movements, while the Soviet-sponsored Czech security police visited their homes and called several in for questioning.

One would have supposed that those Western intellectuals

and journalists who usually make a meal out of the pleas of 'dissidents' would have responded instantly to what their colleagues in Prague were saying. Or perhaps – if one follows my arguments as to the functions of the Cold War – one would not suppose so, in which case one would be right. The Prague Appeal was not the proper stereotyped script of what 'dissidents' are supposed to say. (They were supposed to welcome modern NATO missiles pointed at their cities, which in some never-explained way were to be a promise of freedom.) It is more surprising that a dwindling number of pro-Soviet acrobats in the peace movement chose to turn away from the Appeal, since it confused their muddled view of 'detente' (exclusively with the established authorities) and they didn't wish to be seen talking to 'dissidents'.

And who are these terrible 'dissidents'? Several, like Konrád and Havel, are writers with an international reputation. Others – Andras Hegedüs and Jiri Hayek (Dubcek's Foreign Minister) – are former members of government. Charter 77 is a quite remarkable circle of persons, of widely varying views and beliefs – former Communists of Dubcek's time, Protestant pastors, Catholic intellectuals, liberals, socialists and even (it is rumoured) one or two Trotskyists – women and men of many professions and occupations, united in their defence of human rights. Dr Jaroslav Šabata, a philosopher and psychologist, joined the Communist Party in 1947 and was a member of its Central Committee just after the Prague Spring. Expelled from the party in 1971, he distributed leaflets in a ritual 'election', advising citizens of their right not to vote. The reward for this was a sentence of six and a half years' imprisonment. Released at the end of 1976, he was one of the first signatories of Charter 77. Imprisoned again in 1978, for meeting on the border with Polish KOR activists, he was released after two years when several heart attacks forced him to retire. Perhaps the security services supposed that he was finished. He was not. He continues to speak to us.

There are other 'dissidents' among these peaceniks who are scarcely less terrible. There are Olga and Yuri Medvedkov in Moscow, geographers with an international reputation, who continue cheerfully to welcome Western peace visitors (including Joan Ruddock and Bruce Kent) to their flat, after five years' non-stop harassment and surveillance. As I write I learn that Yuri has just been released after two weeks of hunger strike during yet one more brief sentence as a 'hooligan'! I am ashamed that I can do little more in the way of solidarity than exchange with him photographs of our cats. (He has a fine cat called Tiger, who is also under surveillance by the KGB as a potential holigan.)[9] There is also that well-known 'agent of Western imperialism', Ladislav Lis, who, when Soviet tanks entered Prague in 1968, organized the underground Congress of the Czechoslovak Communist Party in a factory a few hundred yards from their guns. He was a spokesperson for Charter 77 in 1982, and was imprisoned for entering into correspondence with the Western peace movement. In fact, his offence on the court record was far worse. He has a smallholding in the country, and several of his sheep were arrested as hooligans for trespassing without Party cards on common land. Now out of prison, Lis also signed the Prague Appeal.

If people with this courage and integrity reach out their hands to us and ask us to join in a common effort to overthrow the whole Cold War system, do they not deserve our response?

Those are unofficial voices, to be sure: mere 'dissidents'. But almost everything worth anything in the world was first placed on the agenda by 'dissidents' and unofficial groups. (The Western peace movement is made up of the same stuff.) These are the people who may first see the way through the blockades which the past has placed in the future's way.

Political leaders – even 'modernizers' and reformers – will be more circumspect. They will not wish to give one inch of advantage away to the other side. Yet it has become apparent to us that even in the Communist bureaucracies there are people who are now willing to discuss, very cautiously, some new kind of compromise: zones of disengagement, mutual security arrangements, a 'trade-off' in nuclear weapons. From Brezhnev to Andropov the Soviet leadership was obsessed with the superpower Other and talked to the United States above the heads of the rest of the world. Mr Gorbachov's new team are more attentive to Europeans and Asians.[10] There is even some movement in conventional-weapons talks.

This is not much. But it suggests that, even in immediate and realistic terms, there is a new space to be explored. I suggested earlier in this chapter that the armourers and the disarmers of the world are now at a point of stalemate. When Mrs Thatcher is ushered out by the electorate, it could be in the power of any new British government to break that stalemate.

Of course, Britain on her own cannot restructure relations between the blocs nor force the superpowers to disarm. Nor will necessary and honest measures of independent nuclear disarmament – sending back cruise missiles, closing U S bases on this island, and cancelling Trident – have any substantial effect upon the 'nuclear balance' between the giants. It will not even matter very much, unless as a sop to domestic opinion, if a British Foreign Secretary extracts from the Soviet military some *quid pro quo* in exchange, such as the dismantling of a few score SS-20s.

Yet if my analysis is correct, the symbolic political effect of these measures could be profound, for the weapons and bases are there on our territory precisely as symbols of U S hegemony and of Britain's submissive status within the controlling Cold War system. Their expulsion would be the first major fracture in that system. It would be met by a political and ideological hullabaloo many times louder than was visited upon New Zealand for her courageous refusal of visits from nuclear-armed warships.

Indeed, we should expect it to be met with hullabaloo well in advance of the election. William Morris once spoke in a lecture of 'the strength of that tremendous organization under which we live . . . Rather than lose anything which really is its essence, it will pull the roof of the world down upon its head.' It is likely that the tremendous organization which is NATO will regard US nuclear bases in Britain as of its 'essence'. There has been forty years of investment, not just in hardware and runways, and not only in military strategies, but in the ideology and diplomacies of Atlanticism and perpetual 'deterrence' which put the bases there.

Moreover, the leaders of NATO are obsessed with a domino theory of politics, just as the Soviet leaders were when they witnessed the advance of Polish Solidarity. And in both cases they may be right. A British example would call forth support throughout the world's peace movements. If it was synchronized with initiatives of a similar order from other European nations, we would enter within months up on a fluid world of plural diplomacies.

What forms this hullabaloo may take it is not easy to predict. One should note the extraordinary exertions of the agencies of 'the Free West', by economic inducements (and the threat of something like sanctions), by scare stories and flattery, to induce their Spanish people to change their mind on the eve of the NATO referendum. Students of form may gain some premonition of possible tactics from the last British general election. The media will do all in their power to set the opposition parties at odds. Dr Owen and Mr Steel will be set at each other. Something called 'unilateral*ism*' – as if a tactic of independent initiatives could be an *ism*! – will be wheeled on again, signifying surrender of our way of life. Everything possible will be done, perhaps with more outside inspiration than dogmatic zealots realize, to stir up some rancorous dispute within the Labour Party and to project its image to the public as 'a Row'. There are likely also to be premonitions of the economic punishments to come if the electorate should disobey Big Brother. (The funnel for dollar transactions with Europe might be moved from the City of London to Zürich?) There might even be some little warlike scare – the sudden unmasking of spies or a CIA report on new Soviet missiles.

If the electorate should persist in its disaffected courses, this will be nothing to the hullabaloo which would follow on a new government's election. In our view a peace-minded government – let us say, a Labour government – could only stand up against that if it had an affirmative foreign policy to match its defence policies, if it explained this policy to the public, and if it actively looked out for allies in the world.

Such a policy must include a new *Ostpolitik* – that is, an active diplomacy opening new spaces towards the Communist bloc. The closure of nuclear bases might be unilateral, but the diplomacy must be bilateral or multilateral. And the exchanges need not always be in the same kind: why not trade three oranges for three lemons, instead of asking for three oranges back? That is, we should look for *political* exchanges which soften the edges of the blocs, not just for a swap in hardware. When we get rid of cruise missiles we should press the Soviet Union to withdraw their newly established nuclear armoury from Czechoslovakia and the GDR. When we expel all US nuclear bases we should call on the USSR to commence withdrawing the conventional forces which have been, since 1968, in 'temporary' occupation of Czechoslovakia.[11]

That is the kind of swap that would symbolize a thaw in the Cold War: a first essay in trust. The message would spread through West and East, and each new essay in disengagement would be easier to take. I think it is in the power of Britain to break the Cold War stalemate, not because – after two terms of Mrs Thatcher – Britain qualifies as the moral leader of anything, but for other reasons.

First, precisely because we are at the point of stalemate. New Zealand or Greece do not have the weight to tip the scales, but a middle-sized power – Britain or West Germany – could do it. Second, because of a weight of inherited history – a history which sometimes seems to smother us with inertia or guilt, but which on this occasion might serve to furnish us with resources in a crisis.

History has left us uncertainly at a crossroads, between Europe, the United States (with whom we share a language) and a former empire, which even Mrs Thatcher has been unable to drive out of the Commonwealth. These conjunctions offer us a mediating role, in which several of our Commonwealth partners (India, Tanzania, Canada) have more experience than ourselves. And despite Britain's role as an architect of NATO, we might prove to be acceptable – and more acceptable than West Germany – as a mediator to the Soviet bloc. For the memory of the Second World War remains traumatic over there, and it has not been forgotten that we were once allies. As for the United States, whatever hullabaloo goes on in NATO, the alliance between our peace movements and democratic forces is strong enough to take the strain.

The opportunity is there. Perhaps we will be cheated of it once again, or miss it in the midst of our parochial quarrels. Yet even so that is not the end of the matter. If the Cold War is to be ended this will be registered by the actions and agreements of states. But opinion must go ahead of statecraft: the politicians and bureaucracies are those most trammelled by the past, the last to make a move. The healing of human culture – the response to those terrible 'dissidents' on the other side – is a work far wider than politics. It is wider even than the work of those who join peace movements. It is, at the end of this fearsome century, the most important duty of humans, since it is to recreate, out of the fractured image of two barbaric antagonists, the image of humanity.

Notes

1. For the tangled history of relations between Eastern and Western peace movements, see my *Double Exposure*, London, Merlin Press, 1985.
2. Michael Howard, *The Causes of Wars*, Maurice Temple Smith, 1983, p. 26. I have drawn in the next pages on my essay, 'The reasons of the Yahoo', in the *Yale Review*, Summer 1986.
3. Warren Susman, *Culture as History*, New York, 1985.
4. Herbert G. Gutman, *Work, Culture and Society in Industrializing America*, New York, Knopf, 1976, p. 72.
5. George Konrád, *Antipolitics*, 1984.
6. Andras Hegedüs, 'Going beyond bloc ideology', *END Journal*, Summer 1986 and December 1986 (in two parts).

7. Dr Šabata's 'Letter' is in *Voices from Prague*, END/Palach Press, 1983.

8. Copies of letters exchanged with Charter 77 are available from the Palach Press and from CND's International Department. END office (11 Goodwin Street, London N4) can supply copies of the Prague Appeal.

9. After I wrote this Olga and Yuri Medvedkov were expelled from the Soviet Union (October 1986). And I learn that Tiger has died.

10. When Mr Gorbachov had dinner with President Mitterand in Paris in July 1986 he courted European opinion, taking over the language of the West European peace movement: 'It is necessary to get rid of the political thinking that views Europe as a "theatre of operations". Europe must set an example of co-existence among sovereign, different but peaceful countries aware of their interdependence and building their relations on trust.' It was 'time for Europeans to become masters of their destiny', ridding themselves of the burden of armaments 'from the Atlantic to the Urals': *The New York Times*, 8 July 1986.

11. On 20 August 1985 Charter 77 in a measured statement called for the withdrawal of Soviet troops, or at least their reduction, as 'an exemplary unilateral step towards military disengagement' and as a contribution to the 'process of ending the bloc division of Europe'.

In 1980, some of the authors of the essays in this book joined others in drafting the Appeal for European Nuclear Disarmament, whose opening sentence described the 1980s as 'the most dangerous decade in human history'.[1] The dangers which we saw gathering then, and which in the intervening years have been countered only by the peace movements, are the result of a unique set of circumstances.

The first of these, of course, is the accumulation of armaments of unprecedented destructive power, especially nuclear weapons. NATO's December 1979 decision to deploy ground-launched cruise and ballistic Pershing II missiles in Western Europe brought home to many people a full sense of the danger of nuclear war. In response, a strong – though ultimately not strong enough – movement of opposition emerged. But these two types of missile will number, when deployment is completed, only 572, each carrying a single warhead. Most estimates put the total number of nuclear warheads worldwide in the region of 50,000 or more. Even before the theory of 'nuclear winter' proposed that one effect of a major nuclear war would be to blot out the sun's warmth by smoke and debris, leading to catastrophic reductions in temperature, crop failures and mass starvation, it was clear that nuclear war could reduce Europe and the superpowers to cinder-heaps, and directly or indirectly inflict terrible casualties and destruction throughout the rest of the world.

The mere existence of nuclear weapons, however, is not the only problem. The superpowers are pursuing new development programmes in each and every aspect of their respective nuclear arsenals.[2] One major theme of these programmes is increasing accuracy. As has been argued time and again over the past several years, this is strategically most relevant when the aim of nuclear war-planning is to find ways of winning. This is decisively different from deterrence as most people understand it. In the popular view, nuclear deterrence means having the capacity to strike back after a nuclear attack, the ability to inflict enormous, punitive damage on the opposing side, in the hope and belief that this threat will deter attack. It is not about winning – it is about punishment. For the nuclear destruction of an urban society, great accuracy is not needed.

If the nuclear arms race occurred in the absence of refinements in strategic planning, the increased accuracy of the weapons might be a superficial factor of little importance. Such complacency is untenable. Strategic planning is constantly refined, and consistently in the direction of utilizing the greater accuracy of nuclear weapons to make the impossible come true – to make the prospect of nuclear victory realizable.

In the 1980s, the arms race has been accompanied by a new Cold War between the USA and the USSR. This is the first time we have seen this dangerous partnership. The first Cold War in the wake of the Second World War came at the dawn of the new nuclear age. Until 1949, only the USA had the capacity to make nuclear weapons; in that year, the USSR conducted its first nuclear weapon test. Even so, the USA held an effective strategic monopoly throughout the 1950s. By the time the USSR began to develop the ability to deliver a major nuclear strike on the USA, the first Cold War had gone, replaced by a period of changing relations, which produced nevertheless many perilous moments, including the confrontations in Berlin in the late 1950s, the building of the Berlin wall and the 1962 Cuba missile crisis. The most intense period of the arms race followed in the 1970s: in the first half of the decade, the number of US strategic warheads leaped upwards; in the second half, it was the USSR's turn. Yet that was also the period of detente, when, especially until the middle of the decade, US–Soviet relations were as warm as they have ever been.

Detente was a fragile bloom. It became a cliché to comment that political detente needed a military corollary. It never got one. From 1977 it began to suffer from a series of niggling tit-for-tat actions by each side. It came under increasing pressure from conservative circles, especially in the USA. By the time Ronald Reagan was elected US President in November 1980, it was dead and buried.

Multiplying the dangers of the arms race and the Cold War is the new interventionism. From 1975, when the US defeat in Indo-China was made final, and primarily because of the experience of those wars, public opinion in the USA was for several years unwilling to countenance new military adventures abroad. The USSR, having sent large-scale aid to North Vietnam, provided significant logistical support to Cuban forces assisting the governments of Angola and Ethiopia. In December 1979, Soviet combat forces were committed outside the Warsaw Pact countries for the first time with the invasion of Afghanistan. There was immediately renewed talk in the USA of the need to break the bonds which tied the public memory to humiliation in Vietnam. In 1981, US naval aircraft shot down two Libyan aircraft in the Gulf of Sirte. In 1983, American forces invaded Grenada in the Caribbean and entered the Lebanon, ostensibly as a 'peace-keeping' force, despite the way in which naval forces shelled land targets. In 1986, the US navy and Libya clashed again and then came the bombing raid on Libya. And throughout the period of Reagan's presidency, military aid to El Salvador has been increased, while growing pressure has been exerted against Nicaragua – including economic and political pressure, military shows of strength, aid to the contra rebels, and mining of Nicaraguan harbours.

The Onset of the New Cold War

In NATO countries, the commonest – and the official – explanation for the coming of the new Cold War places the blame on the USSR. The invasion of Afghanistan with 80,000 troops at the end of 1979 is particularly singled out. Even those who do not argue either that it represented an increased threat to Western Europe, or that it was intended merely to serve as a springboard for further moves against Pakistan or the Gulf, are prone to seeing it as the latest of a series of increasingly bold Soviet moves in the Third World – from the support of Cuban proxies in Angola and Ethiopia to the commitment of combat troops to action in Afghanistan. Indeed, the invasion came in a part of the world designated by Carter's National Security Adviser, Zbigniew Brzezinski, as the 'arc of crisis' – the arc stretched from Afghanistan through South Yemen to Ethiopia – where US policy had suffered a series of reversals in the late 1970s. This, it is argued, following years of military build-up while the USA remained quiescent, hobbled by the memory of Vietnam and not in a mood to increase military spending, necessarily called forth a militant response from the West.

The key issue in distinguishing how and why the new Cold War started is an assessment of where the major shifts in policy lay, for it did not just happen along: it was created – the result, even if unintended, of changes in policy.

In the period around the turn of the decade into the 1980s, Soviet policy in most fields was inert. The same policies which had been pursued in the past ten years were still being followed. The end of the Brezhnev era was approaching, but until the man who had dominated the Soviet state since the mid-1960s died, there could be no new directions. This is as true in foreign and military affairs as in domestic and economic policy. Indeed, the Brezhnev era did not truly end until the death of two successors – Andropov and Chernenko – and the appointment of Mikhail Gorbachov as Soviet party leader in early 1985. In that sense, the invasion of Afghanistan stands out as an exception to the pattern, not as its culmination, nor as a major landmark on a longer road.

On the other hand, major policy changes are to be found on the US side, many of the most important ones pre-dating both the invasion of Afghanistan and the election of Reagan as President. In 1977, President Carter gained the agreement of the other NATO states to a target for military spending of 3 per cent annual increases for five years. In that year also, the process began which led in December 1979 to the announcement of the decision to deploy cruise and Pershing II missiles in Western Europe. In summer 1979, the USA and USSR signed a Strategic Arms Limitation agreement and within months it was clear that it would only gain ratification in the US Senate with the greatest difficulty. In the end, President Carter saved himself a major political embarrassment by withdrawing it from the Senate in the aftermath of the Soviet invasion of Afghanistan. By then, the Carter administration was proceeding with several new weapons programmes and a major increase in military spending.

In other words, passing a series of milestones along the way, a prolonged phase of major policy changes had commenced before the USSR sent its forces into Afghanistan.

How then should we understand the invasion? First and foremost, it is to be condemned. That it has been exploited for propaganda purposes by the cold warriors of the West is no reason or excuse for not condemning it. The USSR's explanation that it was invited in by the legitimate government does not stand up for a second: the head of that government was assassinated at the moment of invasion. A new leader was brought in from exile in Eastern Europe. The invasion escalated an already bloody civil war to new levels of brutality.

There is no need, however, to dress this condemnation up into an accusation that Afghanistan was but a step on the way to yet greater prizes in order to explain it. The pre-invasion government was at the point of collapse. Soviet advisers were attached to every ministry but were powerless to win either the war or the support of the people for the government's programme of reforms. Thus, in a process not dissimilar to the USA's step-by-step deeper involvement in South Vietnam in the 1960s, it was eventually decided in Moscow to send in the army and place a more compliant leader in power in Afghanistan.

That is, the decision to invade Afghanistan was a decision about Afghanistan – not Pakistan, not the Gulf, not Western Europe, nor even detente. For long after the decisive interment of detente, the Soviet leadership continued to talk and behave as if it still existed. While Reagan and Carter tried to out-hawk each other in the 1980 presidential election campaign, Soviet leaders calmly and mistakenly awaited the return to more 'realistic' (as they put it) policies in Washington.

The effect of the invasion, however, was predictable. In 1979 few better Christmas presents could have been given to the opponents of detente and the Strategic Arms Limitation agreement, to the armourers and the Pentagon, than a Soviet invasion of a country in which the USA had no economic or political interest. Anyone who took a passing glance at the American political scene in 1979 – anyone who recalled, for example, how a Soviet brigade which had been in Cuba for twenty years was suddenly advanced as a reason for not ratifying the arms agreement – would have known immediately what the effect would be.

It is possible that the Soviet leaders were simply unaware of this – that they lacked adequate intelligence about US politics. Or they may have been aware of it, and went ahead with the invasion because they didn't care about its effect on detente. Or perhaps, in the wake of NATO's December 1979 decision to deploy cruise and Pershing II missiles in Western Europe, they thought detente was already dead and didn't mind burying it. But perhaps the most convincing explanation is that the hard men momentarily gained the upper hand, that in an inert and largely decrepit leadership, and in the immediate aftermath of NATO's cruise and Pershing II decision, nobody could think of a very good reason for not going ahead.

Even though the Soviet leadership has changed since then, each of these possible explanations of the Afghanistan invasion carries its own worrying implications for Soviet behaviour in a future crisis with the USA. For humankind's fate is subject not only to the vagaries of political fortunes and moods in the USA, of which we get reasonable fore-warning, but also to similar vagaries in Moscow, of which we get almost no advance notice, partly because the system is not as open to our inspection, and partly because so few people in the West actually understand the system of power in the USSR.

US Resurgence

The USSR's invasion of Afghanistan was a major event which exacerbated a deteriorating situation – but it did not create it. The causes of the new Cold War, like most of the major policy changes which signalled its arrival, are to be found in the USA. By the late 1970s the global US system of power was breaking down with severe effects on US foreign policy – as *Business Week* put it, 'a crisis of the decay of power'.[3] The new Cold War is the American response to that crisis.

After the Second World War, the USA was in a unique position of power. Its troops were more widely deployed across the globe than ever before. Its economic strength was enormous by comparison with the war-ravaged countries of Europe, Japan and the USSR. With the Marshall Aid programme in 1947 and the political conditions attached to it, and with the formation of NATO in 1948, the USA can justly be said to have created the political entity of Western Europe. At the same time, the USSR was creating the political entity of Eastern Europe. Between the two of them, for all practical political purposes the idea of 'Central Europe', hitherto so important politically, culturally and historically, was wiped out. But the USA was more than a power in Europe – a global superpower, and for twenty years, despite the fact that the USSR was always presented and probably genuinely viewed as a global antagonist, the only superpower. Under American direction, a liberal world economy was constructed. As the old European empires shed their colonies, it was into a system of power created, financed and underwritten by the USA that the new states entered.

Only the U S S R, the other Warsaw Pact states, China, North Korea and Yugoslavia were able to stand aside from this world system through the 1950s.

By the mid-1970s, this system of power was under challenge on several different fronts simultaneously. First, though only in military terms, the U S S R had become a superpower of comparable strength and reach. Second, partly because of the costs to the U S A of the enormous military effort required to underwrite the system's stability, economic growth rates were much faster among its main allies. Only Britain, which for too long retained the military apparatus of empire, failed to exploit the system in the same way. Otherwise, Western Europe and especially Japan experienced much greater economic success. One effect of this, of course, was to penetrate U S markets. Another was, especially in Western Europe, an urge for a greater degree of independence from American policy when interests diverged or conflicted.

A variety of challenges came from the Third World. The Cuban revolution, the U S defeat in south-east Asia, the development of socialist states in Angola and Mozambique, the alliances with the U S S R by a number of other Third World states, especially in the Middle East – Egypt for a time, Syria, Iraq, Libya, Somalia and then later Ethiopia – together amounted to a long list of reverses for American power. To be sure, these reverses have often proved temporary, and the alliances with the U S S R have sometimes been no more than arrangements of short-term convenience. Yet they revealed that American power in the Third World was less than all-encompassing. In the 1970s the Arab oil-exporting states first used oil as a diplomatic weapon in the attempt to isolate Israel, and then raised oil prices to new levels, bringing on the energy crisis in countries over-dependent on oil imports. The industrialization of some Third World countries, though generally not amounting to a political challenge to U S power, provided a further source of economic competition.

Finally, and perhaps most seriously of all, in the wake of

the Vietnam war American power was challenged at home, by a general unwillingness to allow it to be exercised in a way which involved or might lead to the commitment of combat forces abroad.

To some extent, American support for detente from the late 1960s can be seen as an initial attempt to come to terms with these new realities of world power. While the 'Nixon doctrine' decreed that in future American lives should be not risked to keep unpopular Third World allies in power, the attempt was made to get the USSR to restrict its actions in the Third World in return for agreed controls on nuclear-weapons levels. The detente policy also responded to pressure in Western Europe, especially France and the Federal Republic of Germany, for different and more relaxed relations with the USSR.

None of this involved any real reassessment of relations with the USSR: the first five years of the 1970s were the period both of detente and of a sharp increase in the number of US strategic nuclear warheads. The retention of the same basic assumptions about the USSR as had guided US policy for the previous two decades is one reason why detente failed. The changes in policy were important but not comprehensive, and the changes in attitude were only superficial. Another source of its failure is that the USSR saw things differently and refused to accept restraints on its actions in the Third World. Partly it failed because most Third World challenges to US power were neither initiated nor controlled by the USSR – a fact American politicians always have difficulty accepting; in other words, to an important extent it was based on an illusion. But in the end the most important single reason was that the domestic American constituency for detente evaporated. By the late 1970s, the economic crisis was biting deep. A sense of weakness was growing and everything was blamed – from Japanese cars, to oil-rich Arabs, to ungrateful Western Europeans, to a failure of national will, to the USSR.

Carter tried to ride the storm that was brewing in the second half of his presidency by increasing military spending, approving new weapons programmes and developing the Rapid Deployment Force to deal with Third World emergencies. Yet he still wanted detente, still wanted the Strategic Arms Limitation agreement with the USSR. The sense of American weakness with which he was tainted was rubbed in humiliatingly by the seizure of the US Embassy in Tehran and the long hostage crisis. There was another political force arising – a coalition between the 'new right', the 'neo-conservatives' and mainstream Republicanism – with a programme for restoring American strength.

It was a two-part programme. The first was to strengthen the domestic economy – the rhetoric of getting the government off the backs of the American people (i.e., freeing big business from irksome restrictions). The second was to increase US military power, discipline the allies and prepare for military interventions in Third World countries whenever and wherever necessary. To gain both the domestic consensus and the international support needed for this programme, the threat from the USSR had to be raised to new levels. Thus, the apostles of revived American strength began by systematically overestimating the USSR's strength and underestimating the USA's. In their view, the USA was now the number two world power. Repeated time after time by men with experience of power and access to the mass media, this gross mis-assessment became the orthodox view. And there is probably no society in the world which is culturally worse attuned to the idea of being number two than the USA.

The Balance-sheet

From the US administration's point of view, the programme of the new Cold War has had mixed success. Military spending has increased, but there is growing impatience in Congress at the extravagance and apparent insatiability of the Pentagon. The M-X missile programme has virtually stalled. Several other weapons projects are not proceeding as fast as was wanted. The invasion of Grenada gave the US

public a taste for interventionism, but the débâcle in the
Lebanon took it away again. Reagan has steadily built public
support for his policy of pressuring the Nicaraguan
government, but military assistance to the contra rebels
remains difficult to assure, and there is still clear opposition
to the commitment of US combat forces. It is likely that one
reason why Libya was bombed in April 1986 was to so be-
fuddle the American popular mind that the contras could be
given the $100 million aid the administration sought, perhaps
leading in following years to the use of US 'advisers' in
support of contra raids into Nicaragua, just as US air power
is being used to batter rural areas of El Salvador.

Belgium, Britain, the Federal Republic of Germany, Italy
and the Netherlands were persuaded to deploy the cruise and
Pershing II missiles more or less on schedule, and against
massive popular opposition, but at the expense of losing
consensus support for NATO policies not only in the deployment countries but elsewhere as well. On other issues –
most notably the gas pipeline to Western Europe from
Siberia, but also on the Middle East and, though quietly, on
Central America – the cohesion of the allies is no greater
under more militant US leadership than it was in the 1970s.
On the April 1986 Libyan bombing raid, only the ever-
reliable British government was prepared to support the
US action, though a couple of weeks later the Tokyo Summit
meeting of seven leading OECD states agreed to vilify
Gadafy and take a tough line on terrorism. New Zealand
dared to challenge the US right to bring nuclear weapons
into its ports and, as a result of public pressure, the Australian
government was unable to help the USA test new missiles.
Meanwhile, what has been one of the USA's most important
allies – the white regime in South Africa – is fighting for its
ugly life as never before.

Overall, this cannot be an encouraging balance-sheet for
the Reagan administration, especially now that it faces a new
and unexpected problem. The administration took office
forswearing arms control and detente. Western European
pressure forced it within a year to open arms-control nego-

tiations with the USSR. Ostensibly, the aim was to reach an agreement making cruise and Pershing II deployment unnecessary. In fact, the USA was undertaking a public-relations exercise to manage Western European opinion and gain agreement to eventual deployment. That this is how the talks were viewed in the State Department is now a matter of public record.[4] When the first stage of deployment went ahead in Britain and the Federal Republic of Germany in November 1983, the USSR obligingly walked out of all arms-control negotiations. Although the peace movements had observed and understood the American manoeuvres, it is probably true that much public opinion was persuaded by the USA's public-relations operation and the USSR's withdrawal from talks that deployment was begun only because the negotiations had not worked. When talks on strategic arms reductions began, the USA's ostensible and actual purposes were comparable to the previous round – only this time US public opinion was targeted as well.

Having forced the degeneration of arms control into a p.r. exercise, however, the USA now finds itself confronting an opponent in the USSR which has apparently learned something and is at least as adept, and on occasion far more so, at the same game. Indeed, there can be little doubt that the USSR won the p.r. battle of the 1985 Geneva Summit between Reagan and Gorbachov. By then, with a unilateral moratorium on nuclear tests from August 1985, the USSR had taken a step which, given a positive US response, could have led to probably the most important arms-control agreement yet. Here the USSR's policy was a matter of substance, not just show: it was a good and positive initiative and the USA cannot be forgiven for having slapped it down – no more can the Thatcher government for having followed suit. Indeed, the USSR's persistence with the moratorium past its first deadline and despite the deliberately visible US programme of testing is the only serious sign from either superpower since 1979 that it actually wants to end the arms race. At the same time, the USSR not only produced the Gorbachov programme for world nuclear disarmament by the year 2000, which received little positive response in the West, but, perhaps more importantly, it was showing a real sensitivity to the issue of verification of arms-control agreements and the need for on-site inspections within each superpower's territory.

So effective has the USSR been that it threatens to vitiate the gains which the USA seemed to be accruing from the Star Wars programme – the Strategic Defense Initiative – to develop means of destroying incoming Soviet warheads in outer space.

Until Mr Gorbachov's new approach began to bite in Soviet policy, Star Wars stood as a major entry on the plus side of the USA's Cold War balance-sheet. There is an almost breathtaking neatness to Star Wars when it is viewed not as a strategic proposal but as a political manoeuvre. It has proven able to kill several birds with one stone. The proposal was first announced by President Reagan in a March 1983 television speech. It was his own initiative, taken without the advice of some key aides and against the advice of others.[5] This is a sign that the President is not as dumb as cartoonists and TV impersonators like to make out, or at least that he possesses an acute political instinct which explains his rise to power as much as does his ability to communicate.

Star Wars offered a vision in which the USA would be safe against nuclear attack. Never mind that this depends entirely on untried and even uninvented weaponry, functioning in a system run by computers which have not yet been invented, themselves run by programs too long and complex to be written by human beings. Never mind that virtually every expert who didn't expect to be employed on the programme agreed that the cost would be phenomenal and the chances of success minimal. Never mind that, whether successfully deployed or not, it would start a new arms race in space and increase tension, not least because the USSR can justly fear it is a programme aimed at giving the USA nuclear superiority. Never mind that even if the system can be deployed it can be swamped or circumvented by cheaper and technically simpler counter-measures. Whatever the problems, costs and dangers, the vision stood – America is the 'can do' country. At least, it was, until the US space programme looked likely to collapse in ruins in early 1986 following the tragic Shuttle explosion and the failure of two out of five other rocket launches.

The US Freeze movement, such a challenge to Reagan and his programme in 1982 and early 1983, found its modest proposal for stopping the arms race and gaining a breathing space for negotiated reductions entirely outflanked by the new vision. The allies were hesitant and suspicious, but could be pacified with the promise that Star Wars would not replace mutual deterrence but strengthen it (even while Americans continued to be told it would replace deterrence), and they could be bought off by the promise of a bonanza if they participated in the research work. Even better, the actual effect of their participation would be to give the USA access to all the most technologically advanced areas of research, civil and military alike. The dollars thrown into Star Wars could also act as a Federal subsidy to troubled high-tech corporations in the USA. Together, the result would a potentially decisive advantage for US corporations in the next round of technological innovation.

Finally, Star Wars provided a way of solving the Reagan administration's arms-control problem, which is a combination of its own distaste for arms-control agreements – and even, in some quarters in the Pentagon, for negotiations – with the fact that refusing to negotiate does not go down well at home or in Western Europe. The ideal solution is to conduct negotiations without risking the possibility of reaching agreement. There is a very good reason why the USSR may well refuse to agree any strategic arms limits while Star Wars research proceeds. Suppose Star Wars worked, it could none the less be defeated by overwhelming numbers of warheads and decoys. Accordingly, the fewer strategic warheads the USSR has, the more effective a Star Wars system will be. If the Soviet leadership assesses Star Wars as a means to give the USA nuclear superiority, and if it cannot match it itself (which is likely, given its weakness in computer technologies), then it has every incentive to refuse to limit, let alone reduce its strategic arsenal, and instead to build it up. Star Wars could thus permanently derail arms control – and thus something first presented as a way of ending the arms race would succeed in legitimating it.

It is scarcely credible, but true, that so many objectives could be met by one programme – beat the Freeze, steal competitors' technology, subsidize U S industry in the only acceptable way (by means of the military buck), derail arms control and, if it all works, get nuclear superiority over the U S S R. However unlikely it is that this last objective will be achieved, the other gains are not slight.

The process, of course, has not been entirely free of difficulties. The allies did not come on board as quickly as was wanted: the initial three-month deadline set in early 1985 was long past by the time the first ally – Britain, predictably enough – had signed a research agreement. Some countries – though the least important ones technologically – refused to participate at all. But in early 1986, the Federal Republic of Germany signed on, followed by Japan. These successes, however, are in the face of opposition which cuts across party political lines in a way in which resistance to cruise and Pershing II missiles never did. There is also opposition in the U S Congress, which has not funded the programme to the full extent. There are many mutterings that American corporations won't benefit as much as was first touted. Dissent on the grounds of cost and feasibility is strong.

Even so, the administration must have been content with its successes, at least until the 1985 Geneva Summit, when the presence of the world communications media allowed it to be made perfectly clear that the U S S R regards Star Wars as the one obstacle to successful arms-control talks. It offered various concessions informally, suggesting it would accept research as long as no engineering development and testing occurred, but made clear that there was a bottom line beyond which it was not prepared to go. In this way, and the problem is especially severe for those who pin all their hopes for reducing nuclear arms on superpower talks, a clear choice has been presented: either Star Wars or arms reductions, but not both. In one go, the USSR came close to blowing apart the p.r. advantages of Star Wars.

I think it is not too fanciful to suggest that this may have been another factor in the minds of the decision-makers in Washington when they ordered the April 1986 air strike on Libya – or at least in the background of their thinking when the decision was made. Something had to be done to keep up the pressure of the new Cold War. If the USSR will not be enough of an enemy – showing the new openness which is a key point of Gorbachov's policy – then there are other enemies who can be wheeled on instead. The new Cold War has not served its purpose. It has not yet succeeded, if it ever will, in restoring US power in the Third World and among the allies, nor in satisfactorily mobilizing US public opinion to accept the full logic of the new militancy. So the turn was made from one hate-figure to another, to a target easy to hit in both military and political terms.

From this point of view, the disaster at the Chernobyl power-station near Kiev in April 1986 is a tragedy of wider dimensions than have yet been understood. The point is not only that it is *Soviet* radiation which threatens people in Western Europe and the USA, as well as in the countries and regions of the USSR much closer to the accident. The point is also that the first Soviet reaction to the accident displayed all the USSR's worst tendencies of bureaucratic inertia, secrecy and apparent callousness, with too little information being released too late.

For analysts of the USSR, there was nothing new in Soviet behaviour over Chernobyl, although the punishment of those who mishandled the initial crisis has been both swift and unusually public. But most people are not analysts of the USSR and set a good deal of store by political images. Cold War imagery of the USSR relates a secretive and repressive bureaucracy at home with expansionism abroad. There is, in reality, no necessary connection between them, but in the Western cultural perception of the USSR they are intertwined. In the logic of the Cold War, the Chernobyl accident has strengthened the grip on our imaginations exerted by the USA's image of the USSR, and in so doing it may have made the policy of Washington's hawks more acceptable. In that way, Chernobyl has increased not only the health hazards under which we daily live but also, indirectly, the risk of nuclear war.

The Second Half of the 1980s

US Defense Secretary Weinberger has referred to US policy in the 1980s as 'the third phase of containment'[6] – a deliberate reference back to the USA's policies of the late 1940s. He sees this 'third phase' as having recorded some successes, but by no means as having run its course. That view seems to be confirmed by the balance-sheet of the new Cold War outlined above. Accordingly, to the extent that the various components of US policy which constitute the Cold War strategy are guided by hands which are rational, or at least purposive, the expectation must be that the second half of the decade will be at least as dangerous as the first – unless a decisive political intervention turns the situation around.

It is, of course, possible – but not probable – that the Reagan administration will be replaced by one which would make such decisive changes in policy that, within a short period, the Cold War would end. The reason that it is possible is that many components of the Cold War strategy are vigorously opposed by political groups in the USA from which a new administration might be drawn. The reason it is not probable is that what the Cold War is really about is the restructuring and re-establishment of US world power. The alternative to continuing with that effort is a fairly open assessment that the USA cannot be the unchallenged world 'number one', that its interests and policy cannot hold sway in all parts of the world, including ones relatively close to home such as Central America and the Caribbean. This assessment, however, would have to be based on, or at least paralleled by, a change of heart which meant that being 'number one' was no longer an issue in U S politics. That is what seems unlikely. It is easy to conceive of an administration presenting a less dangerous and irresponsible face to the world, but much harder to conceive of one which does not try by all means fair and foul to shore up endangered positions of influence and power and to grab new ones as opportunity arises.

What this may mean, assuming some essentially presentational changes in U S policy after the 1988 presidential elections, is that the immediate threat will appear to dissipate in Western European eyes. We shall have less loose talk about nuclear war and fewer efforts to bring the Western European governments into line with yet another new strategic development. But the Third World will remain in the same state as it is now. Non-alignment will be an option the U S A will always try to close down. Pro-American governments will be supported whether or not they suppress freedoms and bomb peasants. Nicaragua will continue to be harassed and the U S military presence in Honduras will not be stood down.

But even if modified, U S policy in the Third World will not only continue to be an immediate threat to all prospects of democracy, independence and prosperity there, it will also combine with Soviet actions to hold the seed of a wider conflict which would engulf us all. As Jonathan Steele argues in his much fuller treatment of these issues in Chapter 5, the only way out of this is to strengthen the ability of the Third World to resist outside intervention. This means both increasing the space for non-alignment in world politics, and supporting particular states threatened by interventionism. For Western European governments to be able to play this role, they must themselves begin an active process of de-alignment, providing much firmer resistance to focal points of U S and Soviet policies, and unhitching themselves from U S nuclear strategy.

The task for Western European peace movements is to combine protest and resistance with a more forward-looking role which creates the opportunity for de-alignment, beginning by putting that approach on Western Europe's political agenda. But it is easier to assert the necessity of doing that than to detail how it can be done, which itself is easier than doing it.

Part of the problem is that there is so much that needs to be resisted. In the case of Britain, we have to act against the cruise missile exercises, the Polaris road convoys, the construction of the Molesworth cruise base, Star Wars, the Trident programme and growing threats to our political right to campaign freely. And there are other developments churned out by the ever-turning wheels of the great military machines to which too little attention has been paid.

Under President Carter, the USA began to put together a Rapid Deployment Force for swift intervention in Third World troublespots. Originally intended as a small force, its target size swiftly grew to over 100,000 men drawn from all parts of the US armed forces. In exercises in the Middle East, the RDF's nuclear element has been made clear by bombing runs made from the USA by B-52 nuclear bombers. All US naval forces for intervention have nuclear weapons, as do the light divisions around which US Army intervention forces are being developed and the Marine Corps units which are involved.[7] The likelihood of the USA undertaking an armed intervention in a Third World region with the intention of using nuclear weapons is rather low. But if the intervention forces face failure, since nuclear weapons will be to hand, there is a strong risk that they would be used whatever the initial intention. If Soviet forces were in the vicinity, or if the target of US intervention were an important ally of the USSR, there is the obvious further risk that the nuclear catastrophe would grow and engulf the whole world.

On another front, US Navy Secretary John Lehman has stated that US submarines would attack Soviet missile-carrying submarines in the Barents Sea and the Sea of Okhotsk 'in the first five minutes of nuclear war'.[8] These are the areas – respectively to the north of Norway and off the eastern coast of the USSR – where the bulk of Soviet sea-based nuclear missiles are deployed. These are the weapons of last resort, the hitherto invulnerable ultimate insurance against nuclear attack. When the readiness and ability to strike at those forces is combined with nuclear warheads accurate enough to destroy Soviet land-based intercontinental missiles, and since there is not much Soviet strategic bomber force to worry about, it is hard to avoid the conclusion that it is part of developing the ability to launch a nuclear first strike. If Star Wars were to work – if it could destroy, not the full weight of a Soviet first strike, but what retaliatory forces the USSR could muster after the USA's first strike – the result would be even more threatening.

The USSR is behind in anti-submarine warfare, and lacks the USA's easy access to open seas; it cannot pose a similar threat to US missile-firing submarines. Perhaps with the thought that Star Wars *might* work and that it probably couldn't match it for some time, if ever, the Soviet leadership might well calculate that the USA is making a determined and potentially successful effort to regain the nuclear superiority it had in the 1950s. In that case, the likeliest response is strength in numbers – more missiles to make an American first strike harder, each carrying more warheads so that more retaliatory power is available even after a first strike, and more missile submarines on station with more general purpose naval forces to protect them from US attack.

In other words, the Reagan administration appears to be doing everything in its power to provoke the USSR to a major new escalation of its nuclear arsenal, reaching beyond its current plans, which are ambitious and dangerous enough.

Meanwhile, in Europe, the USA has been pushing for most of the 1980s for a revision of NATO strategy. Hitherto, NATO's non-nuclear forces have been largely defensive in orientation. The capacity has existed for air strikes into Warsaw Pact territory and, in a relatively limited way, for some ground offensives or counter-offensives. At the same time, NATO's force structure contains nuclear weapons at all levels from artillery and demolition munitions up to nuclear bombers and missiles. As a result, NATO's forces have not had the purely defensive function and appearance that is sought by most proponents of wholly non-nuclear strategies.[9] The new approach, however, places much greater emphasis on strikes and offensives into Warsaw Pact territory. The US Army's Air Land Battle doctrine integrates conventional, chemical and nuclear weapons, and envisages their use in strikes against the follow-up forces of a Warsaw Pact offensive.[10] Under various names – Follow-On Forces Attack, Deep Strike, the Rogers Plan – the rest of NATO is being pushed to follow suit.

It is claimed that the change does not reflect a shift to an aggressive overall strategy. The argument is that it would only be utilized once a Warsaw Pact attack had begun – but that is not so dissimilar to the arguments used by the Warsaw Pact, and fairly widely accepted by close observers, that any offensive operation would only be launched in response to NATO or US aggression. Thus, although the Warsaw Pact deploys heavy concentrations of armoured forces which appear to be designed for offensives, it argues that they are defensive in purpose. If the new US approach is adopted throughout NATO, the position will be similar: forces which look aggressive, but are claimed to be defensive.

The main dangers of these developments do not concern what happens after war has started. Even without the new US naval strategy and AirLand Battle, war between NATO and the Warsaw Pact will almost certainly go nuclear and cause destruction beyond our worst imaginings. Their real dangers are in the period before war starts – intensifying confrontation, making trust non-existent and arms reductions next to impossible, and ultimately bringing war closer, making it less likely that superpower crises can be resolved and conflict avoided. Strategic perceptions are enormously important: they create their own realities. Never are they more important than in time of major crisis when decision-makers would be subject to great psychological stress, clouding understanding and making miscalculation more likely.

All the main directions of US strategy in the 1980s involve military postures which look more aggressive. As the USSR develops its countermeasures, the mad logic of 'retaliating first' may become more and more attractive in either Washington or Moscow or both.

Europe's Choices

These threats cannot be turned aside by self-contained campaigns of opposition and resistance, important though they are. Nor can we afford merely to wait in the hope that the next American administration will ease things up a bit. Even if it wanted to, by the time that happened the USSR may have moved out of the current phase of policy and introduced, alongside its present nuclear programmes, new measures designed to counter the USA's developments, measures which will increase our danger and act in Washington as the rationale for continuing on Reagan's path.

In fact, the option of waiting and hoping for a more reasonable approach to be adopted in Washington represents precisely the sort of thinking which has to be rejected. It is an approach which accepts dependence on the USA, and its hopes for action to improve the situation therefore swing on what happens in American politics. There is growing awareness in Western Europe that depending on the USA is unacceptable. In the 1984 *British Social Attitudes* survey, for example, taken well before the reaction against Reagan's foreign policy in 1986, 54 per cent of respondents stated that the USA and the USSR are equally great threats to world peace. Among those holding this view were 50 per cent of those identifying themselves as Conservative voters.

There are three reasons for this result. The Western European peace movements' most important achievement has been to break the Atlanticist consensus which predicates security on nuclear weapons and on US capabilities. Resistance to cruise and Pershing II missiles, always more than the expression of a fear of nuclear war, was an attack on the heart of that consensus. It mobilized a belief in the need for

Western Europe to move out from under the American thumb. President Reagan is the second reason for the current widespread distrust of the USA – not just the President personally, with his evident lack of knowledge of world affairs, his willingness to use a smile and a 'howdy' to see him through those difficult moments in press conferences when his ignorance is exposed, but more importantly the approach to power and international politics which he represents and oversees. Whatever the fears about the USSR, the USA's greater militancy in the 1980s, its renewed emphasis on pure force as a means of getting its way, its military build-up and obvious distaste for arms control have alarmed a wide spectrum of Western European opinion. The view that Western Europe needs more independence in security matters is now so orthodox that it is reaching the level of cliché.

The third reason is that underlying the appeal of the peace movements and the reaction against Reagan are long-term trends which have, over the past decade and a half, given Western Europe greater economic and political independence from the USA. Indeed, that increasing independence was one of the prime targets of the US strategy of the new Cold War. In this sense, Western Europe's continuing strategic dependence on the USA is seriously out of line with the broad lines of its political and economic development. So is the close alignment with President Reagan that Mrs Thatcher stands for, and it was no surprise in the first half of 1986 that she appeared to be paying a high political price for it.

The basis exists in Western Europe for a decisive rejection of Atlanticism. It is far from inevitable that this will happen, nor is it inevitable that its replacement will be much of an improvement. But, however grim the world seems when we list and analyse developments in strategy and weaponry, there is a real opportunity for change – and the peace movements which have done so much to create the opening can and must be among the decisive political forces which exploit it.

In schematic terms, there are three broad options for Western Europe. One is to accept the reassertion of US leadership, for strategic dependence to lead back towards renewed political and economic subordination. This is where Western Europe began in the late 1940s and early 1950s, when it emerged as a political entity under American tutelage and sponsorship. It would mean a decisive change of course in the trajectory since then, and would be a part of the general restoration of US world power, and thus of the success of the strategy of Cold War. It would mean continuing confrontation with the USSR and a dangerously spiralling arms race.

The second option is a partial break with Atlanticism: of its two strategic foundation stones, dependence on the USA would be rejected but reliance on nuclear weapons would continue. In other words, this option is the development of a Western European nuclear bloc. This option made a significant appearance in the British debate on defence policies in 1986. Some leading figures in the SDP–Liberal Alliance clearly find much merit in it. It would not necessarily involve either the break-up of NATO or the complete withdrawal of US armed forces. But it would mark a greater alignment of Western Europe's strategic policies and position with its economic and political situation, creating a more equal relationship with the USA. It is, however, hard to be encouraged by this greater independence, for this option would mean the continuation of confrontation with the USSR and an added element in the arms race. It might appear particularly threatening to the USSR because it would involve the Federal Republic of Germany having a much more important role in nuclear planning, and could therefore lead to increased tensions and higher military spending.

The third option is a complete rejection of Atlanticism, ending both dependence on the USA and reliance on nuclear weapons. It would mark a major break with the politics and assumptions of the Cold War. It means, in essence, the replacement of the now fractured Atlanticist concensus by a new one based on the peace movements' vision. This vision is expressed in various ways, and its elements do not all command total agreement even within the movements. If generalizations can be made, it is a vision which is about reconciliation in Europe as much as disarmament. It is about being an active force for world peace, ending military confrontation and promoting non-alignment and democracy in the Third World, as much as about avoiding nuclear war. It means assisting states which wish to remain non-aligned to stay free of the polarizing vortex of the Cold War that threatens to suck them in. It is not Europeanist, in the sense of the devotees of the European Community, nor is it Euro-centric. It sees de-alignment in Europe as a crucial factor in creating a just peace, not only in Europe but worldwide. This vision would have to be implemented in specific policies over a long period in the face of intense pressure. In Western Europe itself, this pressure will come from those very powerful sectors of opinion and influence in states and the communications media which remain loyal to Atlanticism, as well as from the USA. Pressure from the USSR on Western European moves to enact this vision will be indirect, and stem largely from much more forcible pressure against Eastern European tendencies towards breaking down the bloc system.

The End of an Era

It is one of the pitfalls of laying out such a broad schema that the expectation must be that none of these options will be adopted in a pure form. Any overarching vision must be implemented in the face of countervailing political pressures and is subject to developments proceeding at different paces in different countries and to the flux of electoral fortunes in each. Politics usually enforces compromise. Yet it is necessary to know what broad choices are available to Europeans in the current period, and it is possible to think about how each choice could be made and what the consequences would be. Clearly, if we are to find a way out of the dangers of the 1980s it is the third option outlined above – the peace movements' vision – which provides the route, and some of the chapters in this book look at its elements in more detail.

Much necessary groundwork for the choice of a non-nuclear, de-aligned Europe has been laid. Public-opinion polls suggest a high degree of awareness about the dangers of nuclear war, even if there is ignorance about many details of its worst effects. They suggest agreement with the contention that military confrontation and the arms race cannot proceed indefinitely without catastrophe, even if the details of new strategy and weaponry evade most people. They suggest disenchantment with Western Europe's dependent partnership with the USA, albeit uncertainty about the desirability of any alternative. They suggest a greater degree of anxiety about the possession of nuclear weapons, combined with awareness of the failure of arms control to date, than commitment to independent nuclear disarmament.

Widespread – if not yet general – understanding of the problems on which the peace movements focus and agreement with many of the most important points of our analysis combine to create the possibility of Western European choices tending increasingly towards the movements' vision. Before that can happen, the movements' campaigns must incorporate the sense of this alternative and communicate it. That this must be done alongside and within continuing campaigns of resistance to the new products of the arms race is clear. What it means is not so much changing what we campaign for and against, as changing how we do it.

One aim must be to encourage political parties which have adopted some peace movement proposals into rethinking the basic terms of security, defence and foreign policies. Various parties have shown some openness to the need for new thinking, but the most creative and systematic exploration of the new possibilities for Europe has occurred outside the parties. This is perhaps not surprising, but it is none the less a serious failure. To be implemented, visions need political programmes; they need parties which aspire to and win power, which are capable of carrying them through, and which think in advance about the possibilities and the obstacles and plan for them. That, of course, is not all that visions need in order to be realized. They need to be supported not only by political parties, but also by movements which are capable of mobilizing and reflecting opinion which stretches much wider than the electoral basis of even the most sympathetic and imaginative party.

The possibility, then, exists. Whether it will be taken up depends on a great deal – including a great deal more work by the peace movements which have done so much to generate the possibility of change in the first place. We may be on the verge of the end of an era. The new Cold War has been an American attempt to restore a system of power inaugurated in the 1940s which was crumbling by the 1970s. The critical problems which this effort has brought on could turn out retrospectively to be the first death throes of the post-1945 era. If we can begin to unlock the nuclear confrontation, much else will become possible – but we can probably only begin to unlock it if we spell out those possibilities, win the sort of popular support for them that we won for opposition to cruise missiles, and elect governments capable of responding to the challenge. There is, as they say, much to be done.

Notes

1. E. P. Thompson and Dan Smith, eds., *Protest and Survive*, Penguin Books, 1980.
2. Paul Rogers, *Guide to Nuclear Weapons 1984–85*, University of Bradford School of Peace Studies, 1984.
3. *Business Week*, 12 March 1979.
4. Thus, Richard Burt, then director of the US State Department's Politico-Military Affairs Bureau: 'The purpose of this whole exercise is maximum political advantage. It's not arms control we're engaged in, it's alliance management.' *Time*, 5 December 1983.
5. *Time*, 4 April 1983.
6. Caspar W. Weinberger, Secretary of Defense, *Annual Report to the Congress: Fiscal Year 1987*, US Department of Defense, February 1986, pp. 27–9.
7. William M. Arkin and Richard W. Fieldhouse, *Nuclear Battlefields: Global Links in the Arms Race*, Cambridge, Mass., Ballinger, 1985, pp. 133–4.

8. *Defense Week*, 30 May 1985.
9. Alternative Defence Commission, *Defence Without the Bomb*, Taylor & Francis, 1983, and *Without the Bomb*, London, Paladin, 1985.
10. *Operations FM 100–5*, U S Army, August 1982.

3 Mary Kaldor:
The Imaginary War[1]

Critics of the European peace movement, especially from the
Third World, often argue that the movement is technocentric
and Euro-centric. Although it is true that from 1980 to 1983
the movement was obsessed with cruise and Pershing II
missiles, it is also the case, I would argue, that the majority
of European peace activists viewed these technical targets
of our campaign as political symbols, much like Gandhi's
salt-tax campaign in the Indian independence movement.
The ground-swell of the movement was a demand for
Western European autonomy from American nuclear strategies; we were campaigning about the political relationship
between Western Europe and the United States and about
the lack of democracy in security matters in European
NATO countries. Of course, many people did put the
emphasis on the missiles, their first-use characteristics or
their destructive potential, but, in general, the campaign
against the Euro-missiles and subsequent campaigns have
been much less technocentric than, say, the American Freeze
campaign.

The charge of being Euro-centric has more substance. It is
true that the European peace movement is preoccupied with
the European situation. But does this matter? Is it not rather
healthy that Europeans are trying to change their own situation? It may be that fundamental political change in Europe
is the most important contribution Europeans can make to
the solution of global problems. Over the past few years,
Band Aid/Live Aid has been amazingly successful in raising
consciousness about the plight of the starving. But, in the
long run, what could best help to ameliorate poverty in the
Third World? Stopping cruise and Pershing and initiating a

political process of global restructuring? Or raising many millions of pounds in voluntary aid?

I raise these questions not in order to denigrate the efforts to raise money for Ethiopia and elsewhere. On the contrary, quite apart from the direct help these funds were able to provide, it was tremendously important in revealing among people living in advanced industrial countries a sense of responsibility for global problems. But I want to put forward the argument that the best way, although not the only way, to discharge that responsibility is through efforts to change our own situation, to challenge the political framework of the post-war period in such a way as to create space for alternative economic and ecological policies.

Europe is the most heavily militarized continent in the world. Soviet and American troops confront each other across the German–German border. Europe is the stage for an imaginary global war which is daily played out in the scenarios of military planners, in military exercises and military intelligence, in the rhetoric of political leaders, in the readiness of armed forces and armament industries, in films, books, and TV programmes. This imaginary war, I would argue, is the linchpin of the global political order which, in turn, profoundly affects both the style and content of economic development. Defying the imagination, finding ways of dismantling the structures of the imaginary war, would open up possibilities for alternative ways of ordering international political and economic relationships. In other words, campaigning for de-alignment and disarmament, for phasing out the blocs in Europe, is also a global campaign. Or to put it in a more dramatic way, the European preoccupation with human survival is not just about avoiding nuclear catastrophe, it is also about avoiding economic and ecological catastrophe.

In what follows, I shall start by setting out a somewhat schematic description of the East–West conflict in Europe and the way in which it influenced models of development. I shall then discuss the growing economic crisis and the contradictions of different political adjustments – detente and new Cold War – to the crisis. Finally, I shall make a few comments about the economic and social content of a disarmament and de-alignment policy; some of these themes are taken up again in Kate Soper's essay.

The Nature of the East–West Conflict in Europe

The orthodox Western view of the East–West conflict holds that it is a conflict of political systems, between freedom and totalitarianism. Totalitarianism is considered inherently expansionist, and it is claimed that only the presence of American nuclear weapons in Western Europe prevents, if not outright Soviet expansion, then at least sinister political blackmail. A parallel is drawn with the situation in Europe in 1939; appeasement does not work and must never be repeated.

The official Eastern version holds that the East–West conflict is a conflict between social systems, between capitalism and socialism, and that capitalism is inherently expansionist. The massive Soviet military presence in Eastern Europe, the buffer zone protecting the Soviet Union from the West and backed by Soviet nuclear weapons, is a way of preventing a global war started by the United States and West Germany. The memory of the German invasion of the Soviet Union in 1941 is invoked to explain the need for preparedness.

Both sides share a belief in a fundamental conflict of systems. In the American view, this is contained by the threat of war – deterrence; in the Soviet view, it is contained not only by the threat of war but also by political factors. But an alternative version would view deterrence not so much as a concept for avoiding war but rather as a world-order concept. The imaginary war, the anxiety it induces, can be interpreted as a mechanism for upholding the political hegemony of the United States and the Soviet Union. It is a way of reproducing the sense of cohesion, energy and legitimacy experienced in wartime. The enemy each side perceives, be it expansionist totalitarianism or militaristic capitalism, resembles the enemy the two sides shared in the Second World War. The memory of that war is kept alive. Europeans are reminded also of the victors of the Second World War and of their own dependence on outside powers.

This concept was captured by George Orwell in *1984*. It is worth recalling that the book was written in the late 1940s. It is often argued that Orwell was writing about Eastern Europe. But was not the book also drawn from his experience of the early Cold War years in Britain? The imaginary war was expressed in the Party slogan 'War is Peace':

War, it will be seen, is now a purely internal affair. In the past, the ruling groups of all countries, although they might recognize their common interest and limit the destructiveness of war, did fight against one another, and the victor always plundered the vanquished. In our own day, they are not fighting against one another at all. The war is waged by each ruling group against its own subjects, and the object of war is not to make or prevent conquests of territory but to keep the structure of society intact. The very word 'war', therefore, has become misleading. It would probably be accurate to say that by becoming continuous war has ceased to exist . . . The effect would be much the same if the three super-states, instead of fighting one another, should agree to live in perpetual peace, each inviolate within its own boundaries . . . A peace that was truly permanent would be the same as permanent war. This – although the vast majority of Party members understand it only in a shallower sense – is the inner meaning of the Party Slogan: *War is Peace*.[2]

Instead of three super-states, what was created, in Europe, was two military blocs. The internal integration of the two blocs was accompanied by the segregation of the two halves of Europe. The *raison d'être* of each bloc was the existence of the other. Concepts like freedom or socialism became the expression of bloc ideology – a more sophisticated defence of cohesion around a group of nations which came to displace, in some degree, the earlier attachment to nation.

NATO was formed in 1949. A collective military strategy emerged in the 1950s and national armed forces were integrated into the military command system. Although individual nations in Western Europe were juridically sovereign, in practice sovereignty was limited in security matters. Decisions about defence policy were, by and large, determined by deliberations in Washington and NATO Headquarters rather than within individual countries. Indeed, for most of the period, decisions were taken with little public debate or discussion. In Britain, for example, the agreements to station American nuclear bombers in East Anglia were made without even Cabinet discussion, let alone parliamentary debate.

It would be wrong, however, to describe this military integration as coercion. It took place with the consent of democratically elected governments, at least in north-western Europe. But consent was shaped by the dominant economic and ideological power of the United States. In southern Europe, where domestic polarization was much more acute, integration did involve direct coercion, especially in Greece, Turkey and Portugal. In recent years, with a growing public debate on security matters, it has become apparent that dissent is much more difficult than consent. On issues like SDI, the Euro-missiles, or Spanish membership of NATO, political struggles have not so far succeeded in challenging the principle of obedience to collective decision-making. Hence military cooperation, even if based on consent, does not necessarily imply the possibility of withholding consent.

The Warsaw Pact was established in 1955, replacing more direct bilateral forms of military control by the Soviet Union. The development of Warsaw Pact military doctrine in the 1960s, and the development of a Warsaw Pact division of military labour, has been viewed by some commentators as a way of preventing independent defence policies, such as have been developed by Romania (and, outside the bloc, by Yugoslavia). In the Prague Spring, military officers at the Gottwald military academy were preparing plans for alternative Czech defence policies. It has even been suggested that military exercises are, in fact, rehearsals for intervention.[3]

A less extreme interpretation suggests that the Warsaw Pact was created as a more flexible mechanism for managing the Soviet–East European relationship in the post-Stalin period.[4] As in the case of NATO, Warsaw Pact institutions provide a forum for reaching agreement or consensus within a predetermined set of assumptions. The GDR, Hungary and Bulgaria are all credited with having questioned the deployment of Soviet missiles in Eastern Europe within the counsels of the Warsaw Pact. As in the case of NATO, reaching agreement or compromise is not at all the same as being able to disagree. Questioning the Warsaw Pact provokes drastic retaliation, as in Hungary in 1956. The need for agreement is predicated on the continued confrontation with the West. It could be argued that, according to this interpretation, military cooperation (as in the case of NATO) is based on the ideological coercion of the imaginary war.

Indeed, the strategies and weapon systems that have evolved over the years serve to embed the imaginary war in a kind of self-perpetuating military practice. Missions, command systems and actual hardware are all based on the scenarios of military planners. In the West, military strategy is based on the assumption of a Soviet blitzkrieg across the west German plain. To question that assumption is to undermine the livelihood and career structures of soldiers, engineers, scientists, workers in armament factories, bureaucrats, politicians and so on.

To argue that the military confrontation in Europe served to uphold the hegemony of the United States and the Soviet Union is not to deny the conflict of social and political systems. For the hegemony of these two powers had a profound influence on social life and served to integrate or homogenize the different systems in East and West. In the West, NATO, from the beginning, was seen as a mechanism for preserving a 'way of life'.

Indeed, Article 2 of the Treaty commits the signatories to strengthen

their free institutions, by bringing about a better understanding of the principles upon which these institutions are founded, and by promoting conditions of stability and well-being. They will seek to eliminate conflict in their international economic policies and will encourage economic collaboration between any or all of them.[5]

In Western Europe, in the 1940s, socialistic tendencies were espoused by nearly all political parties. These tendencies were not entirely suppressed, as can be observed in the development of welfare states and state enterprises. However, they were diverted and channelled in directions charted by the United States. The American relationship served to strengthen weak centre-right coalitions in post-war Western Europe. Even in the case of Britain, which had a Labour government, it is widely argued that the decision to rearm in 1950 was the crucial departure point for post-war British development. As the Cold War gathered momentum, the McCarthyite mood and the manoeuvrings of the CIA contributed to a fundamental shift in the postures of socialist and Social Democrat parties and a marginalization of the left in Western Europe.

But there were two specific respects in which the military confrontation integrated European and American models of development or social systems. One was the free-trade regime on which the Americans were so insistent. The Americans were able to shape the international economic institutions that were established after the war: IMF, GATT, OECD, the World Bank, etc. These institutions established what might be described as a free-trade regime guaranteeing the free movement of goods and of capital. Western Europe did adopt protectionist policies after the war but these were gradually dismantled. The free-trade regime allowed for an enormous acceleration in economic interdependence among developed market economies. Trade, for capitalist countries, was viewed as the mechanism for economic integration. Trade grew much faster than output, and trade among advanced capitalist countries was a rapidly growing share of world trade. Foreign investment also rose rapidly and the big increase in direct American investment in Western Europe profoundly influenced West European economies and societies.

The free-trade regime applied primarily to the products of Fordist technology, in which the U S enjoyed a comparative advantage, i.e. cars, consumer durables, Fordist capital equipment. Advanced industrial countries continued to maintain protectionist policies against agricultural products, minerals and tropical foodstuffs, as well as non-tariff barriers against semi-processed products, which were the main exports of Third World countries. In addition, protectionism on older manufactures – iron and steel, textiles, and clothing – tended to be higher than the norm and these were also likely to be the main exports of Third World countries.

The second respect in which the Cold War contributed to the creation of a homogeneous Atlantic society was more concrete. Through NATO, through the determination of 'security requirements', and through the NATO infrastructure the U S influenced the internal biases of West European states. A preference for capital-intensive military spending (rather than welfare), for oil and nuclear energy (rather than energy conservation or other energy sources), for roads and airfields (rather than railways) was built into the structure of the alliances, reflecting the internal biases of the American model of development, which reached its apotheosis in the military sector. And these biases, especially the emphasis on consumerism, were reinforced by the patterns of trade and investment.

In the East, Soviet-style socialism was directly imposed on the countries of Eastern Europe. Stalinism was the much more brutal Eastern counterpart of McCarthyism. This did not initially involve economic integration, although it did dramatically expand bilateral ties with the Soviet Union. On the contrary, the Soviet model of autarky was exported to Eastern Europe; East European countries were not expected to specialize but to aim inefficiently for self-sufficiency in a broad range of products although the type of production was determined by central planners, who copied the Soviet model. Fear of war, which had proved an important reason for autarky for the Soviet Union in the 1930s, and an important stimulus for development, was used to reproduce a similar situation in East European countries. What was achieved through trade and investment and the integrated command structure in the West was achieved through direct bilateral political and economic relations with the Soviet Union. The Soviet energy-intensive, capital-intensive industrial model was replicated by central planners.

Stalin believed that the creation of a socialist world market was one of the most important consequences of the Second World War. The East European countries, notably Czechoslovakia and the GDR, provided an alternative source for Western technology, relieving the Soviet Union, at least for a few years, of the necessity of trading with the West. Indeed the Soviet Union used reparations, brutally, as a means of gaining access to industrial know-how. In Czechoslovakia and Bulgaria, for example, the ministers of foreign trade were executed for bargaining too hard with the Soviet Union.[6] As the American attitude to the Soviet Union hardened in the late 1940s, so the Soviet Union became more concerned to insulate the socialist countries economically from the Western world. The United States enacted legislation which restricted trade with Communist countries and tried to impose its strategic embargo on West European countries. The Coordinating Committee (CoCom) list of embargoed items is still, today, a cause of considerable contention between the United States and Western Europe. Moreover, the offer of Marshall Aid was linked to political conditions which were expected to be unacceptable to the Soviet Union. For their part, the Soviet Union and the East European countries withdrew or refused to participate in the American-dominated economic institutions such as IMF or GATT.

A remarkable shift in trading patterns was achieved as a result of the Cold War. In 1938, 10 per cent of exports of East European countries including the Soviet Union went to other East European countries and 68.4 per cent went to Western Europe. By 1953, this ratio had been almost exactly reversed: 64 per cent of East European exports, including the Soviet Union, went to other East European countries, and only 14.4 per cent went to Western Europe.[7]

The segmentation of the two spheres of the European economy was, paradoxically, a means of integrating the global political order. The existence of a separate Soviet system did not represent a challenge to the Western system, an alternative example to which social movements could aspire. On the contrary, it provided a legitimation of the Western system, a warning that could be used to subdue and divide social movements. And the opposite was more or less true for the Soviet Union. The existence of the West and the danger of war were used to legitimize the Soviet presence in Eastern Europe and the continued technological emphasis on armaments and heavy industry, and to explain the lack of political participation and the need to work hard.

There *was* a conflict of social and political systems but it was within each bloc. It can be argued that several European countries both East and West would probably have adopted socialist models of development if left to themselves, but they would have been different, pluralistic models designed to suit separate national developments. The Cold War contributed to homogeneity in both East and West, and this made the contrast of social systems more stark and more susceptible to ideologies based on fear of the 'other'. The confrontation could be said to have suppressed diverse social and political tendencies within Europe.

By the same token, the homogenizing tendencies of the East–West conflict limited the opportunities for experimentation in the Third World. Military and economic assistance provided a way of incorporating Third World countries into the East–West conflict. This was not because it created pro-West, or in the case of Soviet, pro-East regimes. Rather, it was because ideas about political power and styles of development based on the East–West conflict were transferred to the Third World.

Through military equipment, advice and training, Third World armies were structured to participate in the imaginary global war – the war that was supposed to take place in Europe (or the Pacific). Weapons like the F-16, the Mirage or the Type 42 destroyer are designed for war in Europe.

Because they are considered important in Europe, they came to be viewed as necessary attributes of military power. In practice, these sophisticated weapons are not useful for internal repression, nor are they necessarily appropriate for external wars in the Third World. But the process of arms acquisition, the institutions created to operate and maintain them, established a set of criteria for military power, regardless of the actual situation on the ground. In other words, the spread of arms, alliances, treaties, military assistance, etc., created a kind of world military order with the superpowers at the top. Perceptions of political power, which may be all that matters, were based on how well an individual country would fare in this imaginary global war. Since the war was imagined by the United States and the Soviet Union, it was clear who would win. By accepting the superpower version, Third World countries accepted a subordinate position in the political hierarchy.

But there was another aspect to the process of incorporation in the Cold War. And this was the socio-institutional bias in favour of particular models of development. The military, in particular, as well as other Third World élites, shared a commitment to rapid industrialization which aspired to the American (and to a lesser extent the Soviet) model of development. The acquisition of sophisticated weapons systems created a chain of supplementary demands for airfields, roads, telephones, radar systems, repair shops, special skills, spare parts and special types of steel and petroleum products. Likewise luxury imports of automobiles or consumer durables created a pattern of tastes which influenced decisions about the style of industrialization. Rapid industrial growth was achieved in many Third World countries. But it was heavily dependent on imported technology, especially capital goods. In particular, large multinational corporations, through direct investment or through a variety of technology transfer agreements, played a key role in spreading energy-intensive and capital-intensive patterns of industry.

As is well-known, this type of industrialization also entails growing disparities between regions, between town and country, and between ethnic and social groups. It leads to the creation of industrial enclaves which neglect, exploit and marginalize the surrounding countryside. Problems of resource depletion, as a result of cash crops, modern farming methods that do not take into account the balance of nature, dams and irrigation schemes, deforestation, or the use of poisonous fertilizers contribute to the loss of livelihood and indeed the disasters faced by many of the world's poorest people.

I am not suggesting that a greater diversity of social models in Europe would have offered alternative examples for the Third World. The choices faced by European countries after the war had to do primarily with types of economic ownership, forms of democracy, and priorities as between warfare or welfare; for Europeans, further industrialization was probably inevitable. Rather, I am suggesting that the possibilities for indigenous models of development for Third World countries which took into account the needs of the rural population, such as, for example, are to be found in the Gandhian tradition, for an economic as well as an ostensibly political independence, were constrained by perceptions of political and economic power which were drawn from participation in the imaginary war.

Detente, New Cold War and Economic Crisis

The East–West conflict could be said to have provided a framework for the diffusion of the American and Soviet models of development. The diffusion process led to very rapid rates of economic growth in Europe – the period known by economists as the Golden Age. Economic growth was also achieved in Third World countries, although it barely kept pace with population growth. But, as the East–West conflict became institutionalized, and as models of development were homogenized, so the sources of creativity needed both to sustain economic growth itself and to cope with the consequences of economic growth – inequality, pollution, resource depletion, urbanization, alienation, etc. – were suppressed.

From the 1950s onwards, US economic growth lagged behind that of other advanced industrial countries. In particular, productivity growth was lower than for any other OECD country. The relatively slow rate of productivity growth was reflected in the declining competitiveness of American manufactures. During the 1950s and 1960s, it was believed that the US could afford the overseas network of military bases, large amounts of military and economic assistance, and high levels of foreign investment, because outflows of dollars returned to the United States in the form of purchases of US goods. As the competitiveness of American manufactures declined, overseas dollars were increasingly spent on West European and Japanese goods. In the 1950s US foreign exchange reserves amounted to \$24.3 bn, while the combined reserves of Germany, Italy and Japan were \$1.4 bn. By 1970, US reserves had fallen to \$14.5 bn, while the reserves of Germany, Italy and Japan had risen to \$23.8 bn. In 1971, the US experienced its first trade deficit since 1936.

Part of the reason for the slow American performance was the fact that it was the lead country. The diffusion of the American model of development simply meant that other countries were following the American example. It is much easier to catch up than to initiate. However, from the 1960s, US productivity growth actually began to decline and not merely lag behind other countries. And this, I believe, has to be explained in terms of the characteristics of the American model of development itself. No model of development is capable of indefinite growth. The markets for American-style products were not growing as fast as formerly. It became harder to achieve improvements to Fordist production techniques. The key factor of production, oil, was gradually becoming more expensive and nuclear energy never realized its expectations. Above all, the high level of military R&D and the rigidities induced by military spending and military styles of technology imposed a brake on civilian innovation.

A parallel process was taking place in Eastern Europe and the Soviet Union. Economic growth began to slow down from the late 1950s. It became harder and harder to achieve what was known as 'extensive accumulation', i.e. economic growth based on incremental additions of labour and raw materials to existing sectors. And yet 'intensive accumulation', economic growth achieved through the introduction of new techniques of production and new sectors, required access to new sources of technology. In practice, this meant trade with the West, since the Soviet system is notoriously bad at generating indigenous innovation. An additional reason for the interest in detente was the extremely heavy burden of military spending on the Soviet economy. Estimates of the burden vary, from 8 to 25 per cent of Net Material Product, but it is much higher than for the United States because the Soviet Union was so much poorer. Although it is sometimes argued that military–technological competition with the West stimulated the general level of Soviet technology, this could not compensate for the diversion of resources from investment and consumption.[8]

The onset of detente coincided with a dramatic shift in American international economic policy; 1971, the year of the first trade deficit, was the year that Nixon and Kissinger went to Moscow and Peking. In August of that year, Nixon announced the end of dollar convertibility into gold and a 10 per cent surcharge on dutiable goods. It marked the end of the Bretton Woods system and the start of what is often described as the New Protectionism. By 1973, all major currencies had abandoned fixed exchange rates. During the 1970s, there was an increase in non-tariff barriers, 'voluntary' export restrictions on steel, textiles and even automobiles, and in anti-dumping measures and countervailing duties. Managed trade, that is to say, trade allowed by agreements between states, rose from 13 per cent of world trade in 1974 to 30 per cent in 1982. The 1970s were also characterized by cuts in economic assistance and consequently a growing dependence of Third World countries on commercial bank loans; a shift from military assistance to commercial sales of military equipment; the end of food aid and the dismantling of U S grain reserves, which led to a rapid rise in food prices;

and, of course, the oil 'shocks' of 1973 and 1979. The US was able to restore its trade balance through sales of food and arms and through the uneven impact of the oil-price hike.

It would, of course, be wrong to make a simplistic connection between detente and the changed role of the United States in the global economy. From 1955 onwards, after the death of Stalin and as the gap between the Soviet Union and its more advanced industrial allies narrowed, the Soviet Union had expressed an interest in peaceful coexistence – the notion that when both sides possess nuclear weapons, war is unthinkable and therefore the competition between the systems must be carried on by other means. The coming to power of Social Democrat parties in north-western Europe in the second half of the 1960s also marked an interest in distancing Western Europe from the more belligerent stance of the United States and in creating space for elements of European society that had been suppressed at the height of the Cold War years. It was not until the end of the Vietnam war, however, when domestic pressure in the United States combined with the growing cost of the Cold War, that this more dove-ish mood began to prevail in the United States as well.

Detente was seen as a safer, and cheaper, way of managing the East–West conflict. Willy Brandt's *Ostpolitik*, which amounted to the recognition of the post-war borders of the GDR, Poland and Czechoslovakia and the abandonment of revanchist claims, paved the way for the Helsinki Act of 1975, which is widely viewed as the expression of the conceptions which underlay detente. The Helsinki Act linked three so-called baskets: the security basket, which included respect for national borders in Europe; the cooperation basket, which included economic, scientific and cultural cooperation; and the humanitarian basket, which included respect for human rights. In effect, the Helsinki Act, by confirming the territorial status quo, was providing space for far-reaching changes in the economic, social and political status quo.

In practice, detente meant much less than this. It meant

arms-control agreements, of which the most important were the SALT agreements and the ABM Treaty. It meant increased trade and various other scientific and cultural exchanges. And it meant a modification in the imagination. Televised Summits, with smiles and hugs from leaders on both sides, helped to soothe anxieties about war, and weakened the belief in an external enemy.

But by the same token, detente was fundamentally constrained. For without an ongoing sense of insecurity, how is it possible to justify the continued military confrontation and how is it possible to preserve bloc cohesion? US and Soviet military spending did decline somewhat in the early 1970s, although the US decline is largely to be explained by the rundown of Vietnam expenditures. Thereafter US and Soviet military spending, as well as military spending by European members of NATO and the Warsaw Pact, rose steadily. As detente came to an end, the growth of US military spending accelerated. The arms-control agreements, therefore, did not halt or reverse the military build-up, although they may have controlled the most destabilizing aspects of military technology. The deployment of new generations of nuclear weapons, the Soviet SS-20 and later the so-called counter-deployment of SS-21s and SS-23s, and the American cruise and Pershing II missiles, could only be justified in a climate of hostility.

Furthermore, the detente mood allowed domestic tensions within each bloc to surface. Tensions between the United States and Western Europe had been increasing along with the new protectionism. A whole series of policy disputes began to come out into the open in the early 1970s, over tariffs, over the price of the dollar or the price of oil, over foreign policy (especially towards the Middle East). Without economic and military assistance, or the threat of military intervention, the US did not have the same leverage in international affairs as previously. And by this, I do not mean a mechanistic kind of leverage, attaching conditions to military or economic assistance or making threats, although no doubt this had some significance. Rather, it had fewer possibilities of ameliorating the worst consequences of uneven development, of avoiding economic or political crises through extensive involvement of various kinds. The U S was gradually abandoning its role as global manager, banker or policeman. Hence, revolutions in Indo-China, Africa, the 'arc of crisis', growing independence in Western Europe and the emergence of new radical social movements all appeared to domestic American opinion as a reproach to the new American posture.

In the East also, detente allowed for greater autonomy of individual East European countries. In some countries, notably Hungary, Bulgaria and the GDR, this allowed for economic reforms and limited degrees of political pluralism. In others, notably Czechoslovakia and Romania (which had a very independent foreign policy), it was accompanied by a domestic tightening-up. It depended on the internal situation of each country. Poland was the most extreme example, for here massive imports of Western technology and an expansionist economic policy were combined with a political situation which provided space for the emergence of a genuinely grass-roots mass movement.

The contradictions of detente were not merely political and military; they were economic as well. Detente allowed for a big increase in East–West trade. This was due to the increased availability of credit for East Europe, both as a result of the accumulation of petro-dollars and as a result of the 'depoliticization' of credit. Western Europe benefited far more than the United States from the increase in trade; in practice, U S trade policy towards the East was erratic during the 1970s and attempts at liberalizing trade were often thwarted by Congress, which imposed conditions such as those relating to Jewish emigration.

The theory was that the East European countries would make use of Western technology to expand their exports. However, this did not turn out to be the case. East European countries had great difficulty in assimilating Western technology. The fundamental reasons had to do with the social and economic framework to which the technology was supposed to apply. Western contractors in the Soviet Union have cited the following reasons for poor assimilation: 'shortages of construction workers, poor qualifications and motivation among those available, inadequate transport facilities, shortages of complementary inputs from Soviet industry (high-grade steel and electronic components for instance) and lack of relevant manufacturing know-how'.[9] This was even true of Hungary, where economic reforms were supposed to have facilitated the introduction of Western technology. Except in agriculture, however, these reforms did not substantially diminish the role of centralized bureaucratic decision-making.[10] The situation was exacerbated by the recession in Western countries and, in the case of the Soviet Union, by a succession of poor harvests.

By the late 1970s, all East European countries were heavily indebted. In the case of Poland, debt service exceeded Poland's hard currency exports. Even today, Polish debt accounts for over half the total East European debt excluding the Soviet Union. Most East European countries began to cut back on imports of Western technology during this period, even *before* the renewal of the Cold War.

The contradictions of economic detente thus parallel the contradictions of political detente. Just as the idea of confrontation cannot be abandoned without profound changes in military and political relations, so economic cooperation is limited without changes in economic relations at home as well as abroad. The centrally planned economies were unable to assimilate Western technology or to compete in Western markets; it is said that liberalization, decentralization and economic incentives are all preconditions for entering capitalist markets. As the share of 'managed' trade has increased in the 1980s, so East European countries have increased their exports somewhat; 'managed' trade, which includes counter trade, industrial cooperation and barter agreement, could be said to represent the Eastern form of trading. In other words, economic cooperation involves adjustments within both types of economic system and dilutes the purity of the American and Soviet models. I should stress, I am not proposing a mix of sytems or a new 'convergence'; I am merely pointing out that the differences between the two systems create more serious difficulties than is usually realized.

The new Cold War began in the late 1970s. As Dan Smith shows, the main impetus came from the United States in the second half of the Carter administration. It was viewed as a way of re-establishing American hegemony. 'Arms *talk*', I remember an MIT guru of the Carter administration telling me at a conference organized by the Italian Communists and Socialists. New conventional and nuclear war-fighting strategies increased the visibility of US military power, and reduced the self-deterring elements of mutual vulnerability, on which detente and arms control were predicated. Wars became fightable and winnable in the imagination, thus reasserting the role military strength could play in shaping perceptions of power. Star Wars is the logical outcome of this kind of thinking. It insulates the United States from global troubles by making America invulnerable again in the imagination. It takes us back to the 1950s, said Caspar Weinberger, when the US was the only nuclear power. Likewise, the Reagan doctrine marks a renewed involvement in Third World crises, while the invasions of Grenada and Libya are supposed to mark the end of the Vietnam syndrome, the end of the era of non-intervention.

The new Cold War was accompanied by a policy of economic coercion – a policy of 'aggressive unilateralism' as some commentators have described it. In the 1950s and 1960s, the US could afford to be generous and create an international economic system to which the élites of other advanced industrial countries could consent. In the 1980s, the new Cold War provided a way of redisciplining the capitalist world in the American self-interest. Reaganite economic policies were characterized by huge budget deficits, largely the result of increases in military spending, combined with monetary targets which resulted in astronomically high interest rates. The US demanded economic concessions from other countries such as voluntary export restrictions, revision of tariffs such as the Common Agricultural Policy, or restric-

tions on East–West trade. Through its dominant political
and economic influence, especially in institutions like the
World Bank and the I M F, it was able to export monetarist
philosophies. And finally the increase in military spending,
especially military research and development, can be interpreted as a bid to confine the newly emerging technologies of
the 1970s, especially information technologies, to the priorities and institutions characteristic of the American model of
development. Star Wars is particularly important in this
respect. In general, it has been shown that high levels of
military research and development have a negative effect on
international competitiveness. By insisting on participation
in the Star Wars programme, the U S is effectively, if not by
intention, reorientating the European and Japanese economies towards military technology, in which the U S enjoys a
comparative advantage, and away from technologies in which
they enjoy a comparative advantage. If this bid succeeds, it
will be detrimental to all three economies.[11]

The consequence so far has been American economic
recovery at the expense of unemployment and/or indebtedness elsewhere. In Europe, both the new protectionism and
austerity policies contributed to economic slowdown and unemployment even though these economies were potentially
more dynamic because the American model of development
was less well entrenched. While the oil shocks did, for a
while, provide a heady sense of commodity power, at least
for a few Third World countries, which helped to propel the
proposals for a New International Economic Order, the
reality of arms sales, high food prices, high oil prices and,
later in the 1980s, the high interest rates, undermined whatever precarious benefits had been achieved from the process
of industrialization in Third World countries. Commodity
prices and markets for manufacturers also declined both
because of the recession and because of the new protectionism. Debt rescheduling involved harsh austerity programmes; in Mexico, for example, the I M F-imposed austerity programme of 1982 resulted in a 4–7 per cent decline
in G D P, a 16 per cent decline in real wages, and a substantial

increase in unemployment and underemployment. Moreover, the debt crisis was accompanied by the food crisis. With the need to increase cash crops to increase the share of a dwindling export market, dependence on food imports has increased, as has vulnerability to natural and man-made disasters – bad weather, flooding, volcanoes, earthquakes and poisonous leaks from chemical factories. The increasing annual toll of disasters – Bhopal, Ethiopia, Mexico City, Bangladesh, Columbia – is not just chance. The risks of nuclear disaster and vulnerability to ecological catastrophe are both rising.

The new Cold War was reciprocated in the socialist countries. This was not just because of the renewal of the arms race and hostile American rhetoric. Soviet armament had its own domestic momentum – something that is recognized even by a number of Soviet writers. For example, Arbatov wrote in the Party journal, *Kommunist*, that one obstacle to detente and arms limitation was the 'self-perpetuating character' or 'momentum of self-increase and renewal' which the nuclear arsenals had acquired. Even Gorbachov, at the 27th Party Congress, warned that 'the situation in the world may become . . . captive to technology, to technocratic military logic'.[12]

In addition, the growing indebtedness of East European countries meant the imposition of austerity policies. Moreover the Soviet Union passed on some of its own economic problems to the other Eastern European countries through raising the price of food and raw materials, especially oil, exported to Eastern Europe, and insisting on higher quality manufactures. Prices were actually increased in the early 1980s in several East European countries, while living standards stagnated or even declined. The failure to fulfil economic expectations in societies which had been led to abandon political hope created undercurrents of tension, most dramatically exposed in Poland. Hence the need for austerity policies, the need to cope with Solidarity, the revival of the Jewish question and of national questions, all contributed to an externalization of conflict and greater hostility towards the West as a way of reimposing unity.

The new Cold War has not re-established a stable global system. In Western Europe, it has resulted in polarization rather than cohesion. This was perhaps because detente had a real social and institutional content in Europe. The rise of the new peace movement in the early 1980s revealed a breakdown in the old consensus about security policies. Bipartisan support for the Cold War came to an end. On the one hand, right-wing conservative parties accepted the militarist–monetarist tenets of the new Cold War. On the other hand, left and left-of-centre parties adopted radical platforms of nuclear disarmament and detente. Centre parties which had enjoyed support during the 1960s and 1970s, veered uneasily between support for a kind of liberal Atlanticism that no longer exists, ideas about strengthening West Europe's identity and a renewal of 1970s-style detente.

In the East, the 1980s witnessed the emergence of independent peace, human-rights and green groups – all of which faced differing degrees of harassment. These groups recognized much more clearly than the Western peace movements the connections between the East–West conflict and their own domestic situation. The peace groups, in particular, were primarily preoccupied with two issues: the militarization of society – conscription, propaganda in schools, war toys, etc. – and East–West communication. Indeed, it is interesting that both the Soviet and Hungarian groups expressed this idea in what they called themselves – the Moscow Group for Establishing Trust between the USA and the USSR, and the Hungarian Peace Group for Dialogue. One young Hungarian peace activist explained, in an article for *END Journal*, that he:

approached the problem not out of fear of nuclear war. But because of the reality of Cold War, which is more hateful and tangible for me.

We have got used to a divided Europe; it has become too much a part of our consciousness, and it does not even occur to us that it can be changed. I am afraid that this already absurd situation could deteriorate further. It would be unbearable to have closed borders, the halt of mutual commerce, hatred, preparation of one side against the other, and a national paranoia that sees an enemy behind every critical voice . . .

Our first documents, which came out after long discussion, indicate that we think of the Cold War as our prime enemy, and the struggle and its style are indicated by one of the meanings of our name, 'Dialogue'.[13]

East European governments, during this period, displayed what one might describe as an almost paralysing indecisiveness, which probably reflected the prolonged succession crisis in the Soviet Union. Both the GDR and Hungarian governments, for example, appeared to be attempting to sustain detente. Honecker said that deployment of missiles in the GDR and Czechoslovakia, allegedly in response to the deployment of cruise and Pershing II missiles in Western Europe, was 'no cause for celebration'. The international secretary of the Hungarian Communist Party, Mátyás Szúrös, put forward, on a number of occasions, the theory that small and medium powers in Europe have a special role in fostering detente and that socialist countries should not always subordinate the national interest to the interests of the socialist community.[14] These initiatives, however, received a setback in 1984 when Moscow vetoed Honecker's proposed visit to West Germany; Gromyko attacked 'revanchists' and 'semi-revanchists . . . of all stripes' and Mátyás Szúrös appears to have capitulated when he told a rally in August 1984 that 'in view of historical experiences, we fully understand and share the concern felt in this connection . . . For our part, we support all efforts and concrete steps to assure that war may never again be started on German soil.' *Pravda* also published articles criticizing the Small States theory.[15]

The emergence of Gorbachov, however, the defeat of the so-called neo-Stalinists in the form of Romanov, and the 'promotion' of Gromyko opens up new possibilities. Gorbachov himself has referred to the Small States theory and is making strenuous efforts to renew detente and to woo West European opinion. What are the prospects for a new detente?

Towards a New Detente

The economic crisis reflects the dénouement of the American and Soviet models of development. Without major shifts of priority, from warfare to welfare and the environment, for example, or from oil and nuclear energy to energy conservation and renewable energy sources, and without changes in the social and political organization of development, it is difficult to identify new sources of economic regeneration. Both societies, in quite different ways, depend on continued accretions to national income (economic growth) and this is no longer possible within the present political framework except by passing on their troubles to other areas of the world. This is the essence of the new Cold War.

The philosophy of the new Cold War is technocratic, selfish and exclusivist. What is deeply disturbing, especially in the United States, is the way in which those who cling to the existing political framework have insulated themselves psychologically from the consequences of their views. Whether it is the high-tech glee of the Libyan raid or the absence of compassion for the victims of Chernobyl, there is a sense of despair about penetrating their political consciousness. It is this insensitivity to the global interest that presages global disaster.

There is an opportunity for change here in Europe, especially West European countries. European countries, because of their subordinate status, are less militarized than the two superpowers. The relationship with the United States no longer serves the self-interest of West European élites. The aspirations for a different set of development goals, which have emerged from new and older social movements, are reflected in the programmes of both left and centre political parties. Of course, among the West European establishments, there are also technocratic exclusivist ideas. Interest in a West European military bloc and in West European cooperation on high tech reflects these ideas. They have reached their zenith in France where lofty ambitions for a European technological renaissance are linked to the generous offer of a

French nuclear *parapluie* for Western Europe. I am sceptical about how far these ideas can be taken, however, because of the difficulty of reaching agreement among the West European powers without the forceful hand of the United States.

The alternative prospect of mobilizing these new-formed European interests around a new detente may seem more Utopian but is, I believe, the only viable alternative to the new Cold War. A new detente has to go beyond the detente of the 1970s. It has to set in motion a social and political process that, unlike the detente of the 1970s, is irreversible.

Above all, this means ending the imaginary war. The East–West conflict does have less hold on our minds than it did in the 1950s and this is why the new Cold War was so much less effective than the first Cold War. Nevertheless the continued oppression in Eastern Europe continues to provide reasons for new anxieties. April Carter, in Chapter 4, sets out the concrete steps which could contribute to a process of phasing out the blocs in Europe. What is needed is, in a sense, a reiteration of the principles of Helsinki. On the one hand, a reduction in armaments of all kinds and agreements to sanctify the post-war European borders, and, on the other hand, tolerance of diversity and pluralism, especially in Eastern Europe. In the last resort, change in Europe has to be tolerated by the superpowers, and the only way this can be done is by convincing global opinion that the East–West conflict in Europe is over. We have to convince the Americans that there are alternative peaceful ways of living with Soviet power and of dealing with oppression. We have to convince the Soviet Union, and this could be even more difficult, that Soviet security is assured even without a Soviet-style socialism in Eastern Europe. The task of persuasion can only be done through practice and this is why creating a social detente in Europe has such a priority.

By a social detente, I do not mean a mix of systems. I mean new forms of economic, social and cultural cooperation that could contribute to experimentation in social and political organization in such a way as to change the goals and content of development. At present, East–West cooperation, especially in the economic sphere, represents an uneasy coming together of the American and Soviet models of development. It is not self-evident that it would be of benefit to either system to increase the mix. For East Europeans, free markets could well mean the re-emergence of inequality and un-employment. For West Europeans, increased state planning could mean the growth of heavy-handed bureaucracy, increased inefficiency and wastage and increased centralization. Yet there are signs in both systems that economists, activists and others are searching for new ways of deciding social goals, of identifying needs and of allocating resources to meet those needs. Some of the proposals which have emerged in Britain out of the experience of municipal socialism in London or Sheffield find echoes in the writings of the reformist economists now publishing in the Soviet Union. There is, for example, talk of economic self-management, decentralization, competitive social ownership and of a diversity of forms of social ownership and democratization (although this has quite a different meaning in the Soviet Union).[16] There are also proposals for direct East–West contacts between enterprises and sectors, that is to say ending the monopoly of the ministries of foreign trade. Building direct contacts at the level of citizens, between professional groups, traders, environmentalists and energy-conservation groups would effectively constitute the process of adapting models of development.

An example of this kind of thinking was expressed by GDR peace activists in their response to the Prague Appeal issued by Charter 77 in Czechoslovakia.

The peace movement must be an emancipation movement in the widest sense. Ecology, Third World and women's groups belong to it, as do movements which work for democratic renewal of society, for establishment of human rights and for an alternative culture, as do social and national minorities. Many goals of the new peace movement are also identical with the workers' movement: the elimination of stupefying work and self-determination in the workplace. The classical relations of dependence and exploitation still exist, although new dangers have been superimposed on them. A form of democratic socialism, freed, by means of socialization and decentralization, from the system of growth at any price and oriented towards an ecological humanism, is conceivable in our two countries.[17]

The point is not that social change is a precondition for, as the GDR peace activists put it, 'a peaceful and undivided Europe'. Rather, the point is that detente must tolerate change, that aspirations for alternative models of development – that are more caring towards the poorest people and towards nature and that allow individuals an element of choice and responsibility for the kind of life they wish to live – should not be suppressed for fear of destabilizing the status quo, for fear of the imaginary war. Otherwise there is no way out. Yearnings for change exist in Europe and the Third World. The refusal to hear or respect those yearnings is what underlies the mad technocratic exclusivism in which the political status quo is caught.

Notes

1. This chapter was based on research undertaken for the United Nations University Subprogramme on Peace and Global Transformation.
2. *1984*, Penguin Books, 1983 edition, p. 173.
3. See Christopher Jones, *Soviet Influence in Eastern Europe: Political Autonomy and the Warsaw Pact*, New York, Praeger, 1981.
4. Gerard Holden, *Division of Labour in the Warsaw Treaty Organisation*, Report prepared for the United Nations University Subprogramme on Peace and Global Transformation, SPRU, University of Sussex, 1985.
5. *NATO Handbook 1985*, NATO Information Service, Brussels, 1985, p. 13.
6. Alec Nove, *East–West Trade: Problems, Prospects, Issues*, Washington Papers No. 53, London/Beverly Hills, Sage Publications, 1978.
7. See Joan Edelman Spero, *The Politics of International Economic Relations*, London, Allen & Unwin, 3rd ed., 1985, Chapter 10.
8. See, for example, R. Amann, J. M. Cooper and R. W. Davies,

eds., *The Technological Level of Soviet Industry*, London, Yale University Press, 1977.

9. Morris Bornstein, 'West–East technology transfer: the Soviet Union', *OECD Observer*, September 1985.

10. See Paul Marer, 'East–West technology transfer: Hungary', *OECD Observer*, September 1985.

11. For evidence on the relationship between military R&D spending and civilian innovation, see M. Kaldor, W. Walker, and M. Sharp, 'Military R&D and industrial competitiveness', *Lloyds Bank Review*, October 1986, and on Star Wars, in particular, William D. Harking *et al.*, *The Strategic Defense Initiative: Costs, Contractors and Consequences*, New York, Council on Economic Priorities, 1983 (plus updated version).

12. For a survey of these views, see Patrick Litherland, 'Nuclear arms: a one-horse race?', *Detente*, Spring 1986.

13. Janos Laszlo, 'I do have the right to make my voice heard', *END Journal*, Issue 3, April/May 1983.

14. Mátyás Szűrös, 'Interaction of the national and international in Hungarian policy', *New Hungarian Quarterly*, Vol. XXV, No. 93, Spring 1984.

15. Quoted in Karen Dawisha, 'Gorbachev and Eastern Europe: a new challenge for the West', *World Policy Journal*, Spring 1986.

16. See, for example, Sidney I. Ploss, 'A new Soviet era?', *Foreign Policy*, Spring 1986; Stephen Shenfield, 'The road to NEP', *Detente*, Spring 1986; Robin Murray, 'Public sector possibilities', *Marxism Today*, July 1986.

17. Published in *Across Frontiers*, Winter 1985.

PART TWO

Alternatives

4 *April Carter:*
The Peace Movement Alternative

Many of those who began by protesting against cruise and Pershing II missiles have become increasingly aware of the need to devise new policies which offer a way out of the present impasse between the US and USSR. Given the political, ideological and national diversity of those linked to the peace movements in Western Europe, there is no single and agreed 'peace movement alternative'. But there is a general perspective shared by many within Western Europe whose aim is to create a new political order which will end the nuclear confrontation between the great powers, progressively reduce their control over their respective halves of Europe and prevent military intervention in other parts of the world. Western Europeans who adopt this perspective have entered into a dialogue with some independent groups in Eastern Europe, and allied themselves with Americans resisting their government's military actions.

This chapter explores policies which offer a coherent alternative not only to the Reagan administration's pursuit of nuclear superiority and world-wide military dominance, but also to the more moderate strategic orthodoxy, which has over the last twenty-five years relied upon detente between the great powers and upon limited measures of arms control to restrain the military build-up. The fundamental requirement is for Western European countries to break away from their habit of automatic compliance with American leadership within NATO, to assert a new approach to defence and develop a new relationship with Eastern Europe and the Soviet Union. Western Europe has the power and opportunity to provide leverage for a change of course, and it has in addition a growing incentive to do so.

In the past Western European governments have often exerted pressure to keep American troops and American nuclear weapons stationed on their territory, in order to ensure Washington's military commitment to them and in particular to 'couple' the U S nuclear forces to Europe. This ingrained habit of relying on American military power and accepting U S direction of the alliance is still evident in the way most Western European governments behave. But there are signs of a growing divergence in interests and attitudes between Western Europe and the United States, even between conservative European parties and the Republican administration.

This divergence creates a real possibility of Western Europe asserting a greater political independence to match its present economic strength – discussion of a 'European pillar of NATO' is one indication of this trend. But greater West European assertiveness is not automatically favourable to peace. If it is fuelled by a desire to recapture great-power status for Western European powers, and is associated with the goal of a European nuclear force, or a major conventional build-up, it could intensify East–West divisions. Creating a stable peace must mean countries like Britain and France abandoning imperial nostalgia and abstaining from military intervention in other parts of the world. The peace movement seeks to mobilize Western European countries to start a process of nuclear disarmament and of reducing conventional confrontation and to seek greater influence in the context of detente and a gradual dissolution of the blocs and respect for the autonomy of countries in the Third World.

Creating a Nuclear-weapon-free Europe

The first priority must be to lessen the risk of a nuclear war. Nuclear-weapon-free zones in area of military confrontation are a means of reducing this risk and of creating the strategic and political conditions for more substantial nuclear disarmament or military disengagement by the great powers.

Even a limited zone, like the 300-kilometre-wide zone in central Europe proposed by the Palme Commission in 1982, would make it less likely that a border incident could trigger a nuclear war, and would slow down escalation in the event of war by avoiding the danger of nuclear weapons being overrun in an attack. But the most significant advantages would stem from a nuclear-free zone covering several countries, and ideally the whole of Europe. The central case for such a zone does not rest on what might happen if war broke out – when it is impossible to guarantee that nuclear weapons will not be reintroduced or used by the great powers – but on its role in ensuring peace. A major nuclear-weapon-free zone in Europe would be a move away from the division of Europe into hostile military blocs and promote other forms of military disengagement.

A European nuclear-free zone would in addition be a stimulus to creating nuclear-free zones in other areas of the world, and would be an inducement to the great powers to cut their own nuclear stockpiles. The U S has a world-wide network of nuclear bases and an extensive nuclear arsenal partly on the grounds that its allies need this nuclear 'protection'. If these bases and the rationale for tactical nuclear weapons were being abandoned, the Americans would have to rethink their nuclear strategy and would be under pressure for deep cuts in their arsenal. The Soviet Union, which has developed its own nuclear weaponry in part to combat a world-wide American deployment, would also have military reasons to reassess its nuclear-weapons programme and would be under international political pressure to do so.

There are a number of steps which NATO could take to move towards a nuclear-free Europe. The first obvious move is a commitment to 'no first use' of nuclear weapons, which would symbolize a rejection of NATO's long-term policy of relying on the nuclear threat even in response to a conventional attack by the Warsaw Pact. The Soviet Union has already declared a policy of 'no first use', but the value of this step has been undermined by the fact that it is not clear to the West that this declaration has been translated into strategic planning. A NATO commitment would, however, have considerable impact for several reasons. NATO has always placed much greater public reliance on using battlefield nuclear weapons than the Warsaw Pact, and a 'no first use' policy would mean that European states were willing to place less emphasis on the need for an American nuclear guarantee. Moreover a 'no first use' declaration would create political pressure for NATO to rethink its whole strategy and plan NATO exercises that do not envisage resort to nuclear weapons. NATO has in fact in recent years somewhat reduced its stress on early use of nuclear weapons to repel conventional forces, but retains the option of first use; and the recently introduced American army doctrine of AirLand Battle, which plans to use nuclear and chemical as well as conventional warheads for attacks into Warsaw Pact territory, undermines the official change of emphasis.

In order to give a 'no first use' commitment real weight, the next step would be to remove all battlefield nuclear weapons (such as short-range nuclear-tipped missiles and nuclear artillery shells) from a zone near the border and to cut down radically the numbers of such weapons stored in Europe. NATO decisions since 1979 to withdraw 2,500 of their older battlefield nuclear weapons have not signified a real change in strategy, since new neutron weapons for use in Europe are being stored in the US. So a real move away from a strategy of nuclear war-fighting in Europe would mean not only further cuts in nuclear weapons now stored in Western Europe, but also an explicit American undertaking not to move them into Europe in time of crisis or war.

NATO adoption of a policy renouncing first use of nuclear weapons and development of a strategy that does not rely on battlefield nuclear weapons are both steps that NATO could take unilaterally, and that have support in quite a wide range of political and strategic opinion. It is much more controversial whether European countries in NATO should move towards abandoning any reliance on the deterrent role of the American nuclear force, and how far NATO should be prepared to go in unconditional measures of nuclear disarmament. There is not total agreement on these questions within the peace movement itself, though there is a widespread conviction that cruise and Pershing II missiles should be removed as a priority, to symbolize European rejection of a potential first-strike policy, and that NATO should abandon preparations for fighting a nuclear war in Europe.

The Role of Unilateralism

The most distinctive element of peace-movement proposals is that individual countries, or NATO as a whole, should take unilateral action to remove certain weapons, or to renounce particularly dangerous policies. Unilateralism has been most central for the British nuclear disarmament movement, because CND has demanded Britain should unconditionally abandon its own nuclear force as a contribution towards stopping the spread of nuclear weapons and promoting nuclear disarmament by the great powers. But unilateral measures are an important element in a peace-movement perspective on how to begin ending the military confrontation in Europe.

Unilateral action to scale down arms or alter defence strategy can take different forms and can be based on varying motives. Unconditional rejection of certain weapons or policies usually stems from the conviction that it is essential to set moral limits – for example, to use of nuclear or chemical weapons – and that a unilateral commitment helps to strengthen existing inhibitions and create an international context in which these limits are generally respected. But it may also be based on a military calculation that possessing nuclear weapons, for example, makes it more likely that the other side will use its own nuclear weapons.

Unilateral measures are, however, usually intended to encourage reciprocation by the other side, by setting in train political pressures for a response, or to influence strategic calculations. Since weapons development and deployments are certainly influenced in part by perceptions of what the opponent is doing, unilateral measures of disarmament or restraint are likely to have some effect on the other side. Indeed arms-control theorists have long argued the benefits of tacit strategic restraint, though they have tended to accept orthodox dislike of public unilateral gestures.

Unconditional limits on arms demonstrate seriousness of intent and invite reciprocation. Unilateral action by one side can lead to a formal treaty, which binds all parties and may include forms of verification. It is also possible to envisage a combination of unilateral moves in Central Europe to remove nuclear weapons, and negotiations to create nuclear-free zones in the Nordic area and in the Balkans, which have been discussed for some years but never very seriously pursued. The goal of unilateral action is to secure multilateral restraint or agreement. One reason for unilateralism is that negotiation has often proved to be a screen for the arms race. Governments may enter into talks to pacify domestic or international opinion with no intention of reaching agreement; and even if some members of governments involved in talks are serious, the process maximizes the possibility for opponents of disarmament to prolong negotiations and obstruct or erode agreement. Theories of 'negotiating from strength' and of developing new weapons as 'bargaining chips' have sometimes served to promote an arms build-up as a result of negotiations. Unilateralism means scaling down the arms race before or during negotiations.

Non-provocative Defence

One standard argument against a nuclear-free zone in Europe has been that NATO needs nuclear weapons to combat Warsaw Pact superiority in conventional forces. This alleged superiority has been exaggerated and oversimplified, often ignoring the Soviet Union's need to guard its other borders, its technological problems, and the doubtful reliability of East European forces. Indeed it has been argued that Western Europe now has the potential in terms of population, economic resources and technology to match the Soviet Union conventionally should it so wish. But it would make no sense to move away from nuclear confrontation, only to embark on a conventional arms race. So it is important to find a conventional military strategy, at least as an interim measure, which will reduce tension and facilitate forms of conventional arms limitation.

The answer lies in adopting a strategy of non-provocative defence. The aim of non-provocative defence is to create a convincing defence against a conventional attack, while posing no threat to other countries. A non-provocative defence strategy deters invasion by ensuring an aggressor will have to pay a heavy price and by demonstrating the will to prolonged resistance. But by concentrating on defence of one's own territory rather than taking the war into other countries, a non-provocative strategy minimizes the fear and suspicion which often arise out of military preparations and removes the incentive for a pre-emptive attack in a crisis. A non-provocative defence policy must forgo weapons designed primarily for long-distance strikes against an opponent (for example, long-range bombers) and especially destructive weapons – like nerve gas – which it would be insane to use on one's own territory. But it is also essential to adopt a clearly defensive weapons deployment and to have an explicitly defensive policy, since even apparently 'defensive' weapons like anti-aircraft missiles can be used as part of an offensive strategy.

The ideas behind non-provocative defence are not entirely new. Between the two World Wars pressure for 'qualitative disarmament' was an attempt to ban weapons like capital ships and tanks designed primarily for attack rather than defence. Since the Second World War the neutral and non-aligned countries of Europe like Sweden and Yugoslavia have adopted a purely defensive stance because it makes most sense for them in both political and military terms. Proposals for NATO to adopt a strictly non-provocative defence strategy were not, however, widely canvassed until the 1980s. Because this approach fits in with arms-control theory, which stresses the need to achieve a stable military balance and avoid unintended war, it has gained support over a wide political spectrum. The German Social Democrats and more recently the Danish Social Democrats have endorsed a non-provocative defence strategy for NATO; and in Britain both the Labour Party and the Alliance Commission on Defence have supported the idea.

Non-provocative defence can be organized in different ways. Some advocates stress the role of the latest technology, which now tends to favour defence. This new technology includes using radar, lasers, sensors and vertical guidance on missiles to direct anti-aircraft missiles, anti-tank missiles and anti-ship missiles against their targets. The Falklands war illustrated the deadly effectiveness of the Exocet missile. But there are problems in relying too heavily on computer-controlled high technology. One difficulty is that in a real battle it might well not work; for example, computers can go wrong. Another problem is that pursuit of high technology is now promoted by the military–industrial complex. So the immediate danger is that reliance on high technology might undermine the political gains of a non-provocative strategy, because it would encourage continuing competition in research and development for even more sophisticated weapons. Moreover, modern conventional technology can be used for long-distance and highly destructive attacks hundreds of miles into Warsaw Pact territory. The latest official NATO doctrine of Follow-on Force Attack marks a move in NATO's specifically conventional strategy from an emphasis on defence at the West German frontier to a much more offensive-seeming strategy, which could encourage pre-emptive strikes in a crisis. The first step is for NATO to abandon this new doctrine. In theory the FOFA technology could be withdrawn westwards and used to create a fire barrier along the border; but this would not necessarily dissipate unease about its deep-strike capacity, and it would be much better for NATO to use alternative shorter-range defensive weapons.

Non-provocative defence can be planned with an emphasis on much simpler technology, using frontier fortifications, tank traps and mines, maximizing the value of natural barriers and relying on territorial reserves armed with simple missiles and artillery to complement mobile professional forces. There is room for considerable debate about the best strategy and technical mix, and about the extent to which some offensive capacity should be retained. No ideal defence policy exists. But non-provocative defence does offer the possibility of a less expensive policy – modern multi-purpose aircraft, for example, can be prohibitively expensive and may be too complex to be really efficient, and can be destroyed by a much cheaper missile. A purely defensive defence would, moreover, encourage some Soviet response towards defusing the military confrontation in Europe.

NATO should adopt a non-provocative defence strategy regardless of what the Soviet Union may do. Indeed the fact that the USSR now operates on the principle of pre-emptive defence and Warsaw Pact forces are organized to launch a blitzkrieg attack into West Germany in the event of war, makes it the more imperative that NATO does not encourage pre-emption. But it would be a major step towards relaxation of tension if the Soviet High Command would revise its present strategy and adopt a more clearly defensive stance. Policy-making circles in Moscow are now clearly acquainted with the theory of non-provocative defence but, given the historical experience which has led to present Soviet strategy and the conservatism of the military, a rapid change in approach does not seem very probable. A partial response, which might be more readily attainable, would be to reduce the number of armoured Warsaw Pact divisions in Central Europe.

Troop and Force Reductions

If NATO adopted a non-provocative defensive strategy, it could explore the possibility of an agreement with the Warsaw Pact to limit the numbers of long-range strike aircraft, heavy tanks and long-range missiles on both sides. This would be worthwhile even if the numbers which were agreed actually exceeded the number of such weapons

NATO wished to retain. At present NATO strategists looking at Warsaw Pact deployments alarm themselves with scenarios of a 'standing start' attack without reinforcements; and NATO governments tend to alarm their publics by highlighting the total number of Soviet tanks. There is scope for a cut in Soviet, and also East German, Polish and Czechoslovak armoured tank divisions, while retaining a reasonable number of troops near the border. The fact that the USSR can reinforce its front line more easily than NATO should encourage Moscow to consider this concession, especially if NATO abandons its FOFA strategy, which is partly intended to destroy reinforcements. The Warsaw Pact's June 1986 proposals for a new forum to discuss troop cuts in Europe suggested that there may be a genuine interest in force reductions.

Non-provocative defence would not automatically lead to fewer troops on the NATO side, since the numbers required depend on the strategy adopted. Some proposals for a purely defensive stance in Central Europe which rely heavily on defensive technology do suggest fewer troops would be needed. Even if in total more rather than fewer soldiers were required by a non-provocative approach, it might be possible to reduce the size of the professional and standing armies designated to NATO, while increasing the availability and numbers of reserves. This could be done by emulating the neutral and non-aligned countries who maximize their reserves by planning to call up all those who have undergone the statutory period of national service and been kept up to date by short refresher courses up to the age of around fifty.

Reduction in NATO forces would almost certainly mean a cut in American troops in Europe. Isolationist trends in the US are already creating pressure for pulling back some of these forces, and greater West European independence and demands for a reduction in the role of American nuclear weapons in NATO strategy would probably intensify Congressional desire to save money on European commitments. Up to now the American administration has always resisted Congressional demands to bring back some of the

US troops allocated to NATO; one major reason for Washington agreeing to start talks on Mutual Balanced Force Reductions (MBFR) in Vienna in 1973 was to head off such a demand. But in the future the administration may see advantages in reduced European commitments, though the US is likely to retain some military presence in Western Europe for as long as it can.

Even West European defence establishments might accept an early reduction in US forces in the context of a comprehensive restructuring of defence, while those in Europe seeking nuclear disengagement and greater European independence of the United States would welcome such a reduction. There is a close link between developing a non-nuclear strategy and cutting down the number of US troops, since almost all NATO nuclear weapons are owned by the US. Although European NATO forces do have access to battlefield nuclear weapons under dual-key arrangements for nuclear warheads, most are deployed by US forces. Moreover, Washington might be more willing to reduce the threat of nuclear retaliation if fewer of its own citizens were at risk in fighting in Europe. A cut in American forces would also mean less American leverage within NATO and could be a step towards American military disengagement from Europe.

Reducing the number of American troops assigned to NATO would undermine the military case for having so many Soviet troops in Eastern Europe, and so might promote a formal agreement to limit the armed forces of both great powers stationed in Europe. In the past the Soviet Union has seemed more anxious at the MBFR talks to limit the size of the West German army than that of the American presence. But if West German forces were structured for non-provocative defence, with a strong emphasis on reserves equipped with low-technology weapons appropriate for defending their local territory, these fears might be defused. Moreover, the political conditions which previously led Moscow to see the US acting as a restraining influence on West Germany have changed significantly in recent years in the light of the new Cold War stance adopted in Washington and the fact that the

Christian-Democratic-led coalition government in Bonn has maintained an interest in pursuing detente.

Promoting European Detente

During the early 1970s Washington and Moscow were engaged in a policy of detente which was based on the assumption that the great powers could, if they chose, co-operate to ensure world stability and should exert the necessary control over their respective spheres of interest. There are several difficulties with this form of detente. It is inherently precarious as long as the US and USSR are locked into a military great-power competition, and when it breaks down the allies on each side are swept into a new military and ideological confrontation. It also perpetuates each superpower's dominance within its own sphere, undermining the political independence of countries within that sphere and condoning suppression of democratic rights. Western Europe needs to pursue an independent policy of detente both with Eastern Europe and with the Soviet Union, in order to create a more lasting basis for peace and to ensure its own political independence.

Development of a more specifically European detente has already begun, starting with a growth in trade but given political impetus by Willy Brandt's policy of *Ostpolitik* in the early 1970s and by the Helsinki Final Act of 1975. *Ostpolitik* involved West Germany renouncing the dreams of a greater Germany and allaying the fears stemming from the Second World War, and at the same time coming to terms with the new order in Eastern Europe. West Germany under the Christian Democrats in the 1950s and 1960s had refused to recognize the separate existence of East Germany and retained its claim to its former territory in Poland; at this stage West Germany often voiced a more extreme anti-Communism than the United States. Willy Brandt and the Social-Democratic-led government reversed these policies: they expressly recognized the post-war frontiers of Europe, renounced territorial claims and normalized relations with the

USSR, Poland and Czechoslovakia by signing non-aggression pacts with each and accorded *de facto* recognition to East Germany. *Ostpolitik* also involved increased trade and other forms of economic cooperation with the USSR and Eastern Europe, forming, in addition, close cultural ties with East Germany and taking joint action to resolve the individual problems caused by the division of families. *Ostpolitik* was a West German initiative, and embodied the goal of loosening the bloc system in Europe, but Brandt's government reaffirmed its loyalty to NATO and accepted that normalizing relations in Berlin gave a decisive voice to Washington and Moscow, two of the four occupying powers in the city.

The Helsinki Conference which produced the Helsinki Final Act of 1975 had been instigated by the Soviet Union, which sought formal recognition for the status quo in Eastern Europe, and increased trade, technology and credits from the West. Although Helsinki included both the great powers, it also involved the neutral and non-aligned countries of Europe and so was not simply a negotiation between the blocs. The 1975 Final Act endorsed and furthered closer economic and cultural interchange between the two halves of Europe and was therefore an element in a specifically European detente, although it also embodied great-power interests. Follow-up conferences at Belgrade and Madrid reflected worsening relations between Washington and Moscow and were dogged by ideological disputes over human rights (which had been inserted in the original Helsinki Declaration by the West). Although the Stockholm Conference on confidence-building measures (such as advance warning of military manoeuvres) that grew out of Madrid made slow progress, the Helsinki process could still be used to promote change in Europe.

Because Western European countries had developed strong economic links with both the Soviet Union and Eastern Europe, a European-based detente lasted (though in eroded form) after Washington had embarked on a new Cold War, and European countries resisted President Reagan's call for economic sanctions after the military takeover in Poland in

1981. The relationship between the two Germanies has been transformed since the 1960s, when they were both intransigent in their hostility to making concessions to the other side, and to each other. Even Mrs Thatcher's government has promoted diplomatic ties with East European governments, in particular with Hungary.

There is considerable scope for extending the links that already exist not only at governmental but at an unofficial level between professional groups, churches and individuals. There is, for example, growing concern in both halves of Europe about destruction of the environment and the hazards of nuclear power and industrial and chemical processes; and a growing need for joint action across national and ideological boundaries. Detente and dialogue between governments and political parties, and between professional or popular groupings, can also play an important role in promoting disarmament. The West German Social Democrats drew up with the East German government a draft agreement for a chemical-weapon-free zone in Central Europe in 1985, which could provide a valuable model for European countries initiating measures of disarmament and exerting leverage on their respective great powers to respond. Scientists in the Pugwash movement started a dialogue on how to avert the dangers of nuclear war in the mid-1950s, and created individual friendships across the East–West divide and made useful technical proposals on issues like monitoring a test-ban treaty. During the 1980s dialogue between professional groups with a special concern about the dangers and effects of nuclear war – for example scientists, physicians and academic peace researchers – and between political activists from both sides, has developed rapidly.

There are, however, problems for unofficial groups and for governments in the West anxious to promote greater understanding between the blocs and to pursue common interests, because most people in Eastern Europe do not see their governments as genuinely representative and feel oppressed by the role and military power of the Soviet Union. West Europeans have to recognize the legitimate interests and concerns of the Soviet government, but should not allow it to dictate the terms of the practice of detente. It is important in principle to support the right of East European countries to national independence and to choose their own form of government; it is also essential in the long run for a stable peace that the Soviet Union ceases to impose military control over other countries.

An immediate issue for unofficial Western groups is whether they should only make contact with officially authorized bodies, or should also insist on working with autonomous organizations where they exist or with opposition movements. The West European peace movements have for the most part had contacts both with the official peace committees and with the independent peace groups that have grown up out of the East German churches and that existed for a while in Hungary; they have also given support to the small but significant Trust Group set up in the USSR, which has been persecuted by the Soviet authorities. The peace movement has had more difficulty in deciding how far to enter into dialogue with opposition groups or movements like Charter 77 in Czechoslovakia or Solidarity in Poland, especially as in the past civil-rights activists in Eastern Europe have often been hostile to the Western peace movement. But in recent years the European Nuclear Disarmament movement has engaged in a dialogue which has created some common ground on the importance of a nuclear-free zone, of military disengagement and of upholding civil rights.

The issue of civil rights inside Eastern Europe and the Soviet Union is exceedingly tricky for both unofficial groups and governments pursuing detente. 'Human rights' have been used as a central element in Cold War propaganda by Western governments that have been engaged in promoting military confrontation and have often condoned brutal suppression of rights by pro-Western regimes. The Soviet government is naturally resentful at the propagandist abuse of the rhetoric of human rights. But those Western governments which have a record of genuine and impartial concern over human rights, and which are seeking detente and disarmament, cannot ignore flagrant suppression of basic rights in the USSR or Eastern Europe. Popular movements that are not shackled by diplomatic niceties have greater freedom and responsibility to take a stand on principle and to demonstrate their independence of the partisan politics of both great powers.

The difficulty of raising civil-rights issues within the context of detente indicates a much broader long-term problem: whether pursuit of detente is really compatible with the goal of dissolution of the blocs. So far detente has involved acceptance of the division of Europe into military alliances and implicit recognition of great-power spheres of influence. Any indication that Western governments were actively trying to alter the status quo in Eastern Europe could prevent relaxation of tension and measures to limit arms, and indeed intensify confrontation. Nevertheless, there are processes encouraged by detente which tend towards loosening the bloc system. Economic and cultural cooperation can promote a sense of European unity transcending the military and ideological divide; reduction of fear and hostility may encourage a reassessment of security interests, and closer links between Western and Eastern European countries could strengthen their economic and political independence. The original intention of *Ostpolitik* appears to have been to achieve these goals. If in the future European detente were accompanied by the creation of a nuclear-free zone and by new, less provocative, conventional deployments, then conditions might exist for beginning to dismantle the military alliances, in principle a goal diplomatically acceptable to both sides.

Dissolution of the Blocs?

An end to the military division of Europe and to great-power dominance is necessarily a distant prospect, but it is important to consider how it might come about. At present majority opinion in most NATO countries is still in favour of some American military presence in Europe and of being

linked to the American nuclear force. Doubts about the
alliance are more widespread in Greece and Spain, and
Western European attitudes to American bases and to the
US role in Europe are becoming more critical. If present
trends continue, there may well be real willingness to break
with the US and develop much more independent Western
European defence and foreign policies – though there will be
conflicts over the direction these should take.

It is likely to be difficult to dislodge the United States,
despite internal isolationist sentiments, since the American
global role since the last war has manifested itself in part by
its network of military bases, and Western Europe has been
important as a military and political bastion. Washington
might be willing to end its military commitments to a Western
Europe still regarded as a reliable ally, but the context we are
envisaging is one in which the Western Europeans are likely
to be seen as having dangerously neutralist tendencies. If one
or two West European countries opted for non-alignment,
then Washington would almost certainly apply intense pressure, including possible economic and political destabilization. But the US is not likely to have either the power or the
political will to take drastic action against any major grouping
within NATO; if there were a strong political movement in
Western Europe, it would almost certainly have support
among sections of American opinion, including Congress.

The greatest resistance to a real dissolution of the blocs in
Europe – as opposed to a formal end to NATO and the
Warsaw Pact, allowing bilateral military agreements – could
be expected from the Soviet Union, partly because it has less
global power than the US. At present Eastern Europe is the
only consolidated sphere of Soviet influence, and it has had a
crucial role in ensuring Soviet security since the late 1940s
by providing a defensive perimeter well beyond the USSR's
own frontiers. These two considerations might be out-
weighed by the potential advantages of removing the American presence and ending the present dangerous and costly
military confrontation in Europe. But Eastern Europe has
another important role for the Soviet Union: by replicating

the Soviet-style Communist Party system of government it enhances the legitimacy of the Soviet government; certainly if the absence of Soviet troops allowed existing East European governments to be replaced by multi-party systems it would be damaging to Soviet prestige. There are significant differences between the present governments of Eastern Europe, but none could feel totally secure if the Soviet Union withdrew. It is conceivable that in the future the Soviet government might become more tolerant of experiments in Eastern Europe, especially if the military confrontation had been scaled down; or that it might decide to cut its losses in Eastern Europe and concentrate on internal reforms. Western Europe could best encourage relaxation of Soviet control by avoiding provocative political intervention, pressing for arms reductions and ensuring that any proposals for disengagement safeguard legitimate Soviet interests.

The most practicable model for an all-European settlement would be for the East European states to accept a Finnish-style status, which allowed them autonomy in their internal affairs and a considerable degree of freedom in their foreign policy, but in which they retained some special links with Moscow. The Finnish form of neutralism guarantees that no military threat can be posed to the Soviet Union from their territory, and allows the USSR some residual rights in the event of war. It might be possible to retain Comecon, at least for an interim period, so that economic relations between Eastern Europe and the USSR were not immediately disrupted.

Dissolution of the military alliances and disengagement of American and Soviet troops might follow from nuclear disarmament in Europe and cuts in offensive arms and troops, but will only occur in response to strong political pressure. One likely source of leverage is a movement within the two Germanies for creating a neutral German zone. The Soviet Union sought a neutral Germany in the 1950s in an attempt to prevent West German integration into NATO, and might see advantages in this approach in the future. There are drawbacks in focusing on a German solution – even if neutrality were granted on condition of the two German states remaining separate, or on the basis of a limited confederation, many in both Western and Eastern Europe would fear an eventual reunification. So it may be more likely that the US and USSR would make a formal settlement of German status and the role of Berlin (legally left open ever since 1945) part of a wider European treaty.

Sources of Change

A strategy for change in Europe either has to operate through NATO, or attempt to disrupt the alliance. This issue has been hotly debated within the peace movement and there are strong arguments both for trying to change NATO from within and for non-alignment as a corollary of commitment to nuclear disarmament and dissolution of the blocs. The case for trying to work through NATO is that this is at present more acceptable to moderate opinion in most countries, that it holds out the possibility of coordinated change in Europe and attempts to carry the US in the direction of nuclear disarmament and disengagement. If a country like Britain tries to change NATO from within there is also less danger of a destabilizing military association between France and West Germany, or of a bigger US military build-up in West Germany, which might arise from withdrawal of a major NATO ally. The case against a government committed to nuclear disarmament staying in NATO is that the American military presence makes it difficult to construct totally non-nuclear policies for Europe, and that the way NATO has so far operated tends to stifle dissenting voices and to prevent governments from pursuing policies opposed to Washington's interests. A country seriously committed to ensuring a nuclear-free zone and non-provocative defence would either have to mobilize strong support from a wide range of European governments or be prepared to leave NATO unless changes were agreed.

So far certain Western European socialist parties are the major parties with some commitment to pursuing the kind of policies discussed in this chapter, and they are still officially loyal to NATO membership. Their willingness to exert real pressure for a change in NATO strategies will, however, depend upon the continuing existence of an active peace movement and rank-and-file concern within the party. Popular demands for non-alignment would be a spur to effecting at least limited steps like a no-first-use-of-nuclear-weapons policy within NATO. If a socialist party comes to power and does genuinely try to change NATO from within, its degree of success or failure will of course influence subsequent assessments of the case for leaving NATO. If an important member of NATO like Britain or West Germany secured substantial European support for withdrawal of battlefield nuclear weapons and non-provocative defence, and the US proved totally intransigent, then NATO might break up and be replaced by some kind of European defensive coalition.

The direction and degree of change in NATO would depend in part on which countries took the initiative. Greece and Spain have the greatest doubts about the relevance of NATO to their particular security and political concerns, and may be most inclined to expel all American bases. They could influence Italy to explore ways of creating a nuclear-free and disengaged zone in the Mediterranean, but are too removed from the central military confrontation in Europe to press for changes in nuclear and conventional strategy there. The Scandinavian countries have always refused to have nuclear weapons stationed on their territory in time of peace and could, with Soviet cooperation, negotiate seriously on a Nordic nuclear-free zone. Holland and Belgium held out for a long time against accepting cruise and were reported to be the strongest critics of incorporating binary nerve gas into NATO strategy, and could act as a focus for changing NATO strategy in future. The smaller countries could have an important impact on public opinion and peace movements in other countries, but to bring about a direct change in NATO policies they would need to act in conjunction with several other governments to force issues on to the agenda. The most direct leverage, therefore, could be exerted by strategically central and powerful countries like West Germany and Britain. The West German Social Democrats have supported a policy of no first use of nuclear weapons and there is especial interest in non-provocative defence in West Germany, which is the most vulnerable country in any European war. West Germany is likely to press for some changes in NATO strategy under a Social Democratic government, but is also likely to emphasize strengthened detente and negotiations with Eastern Europe. A British Labour government on the other hand would, if it observes its declared defence policy, have a particularly strong anti-nuclear commitment. Abandoning the British bomb would not have a great impact on NATO, but it would be a decisive step away from dreams of a European nuclear force; removing American nuclear bases would, however, have immediate reverberations throughout the Alliance. A conjunction of a Social Democratic government in West Germany and a Labour government in Britain would create the maximum opportunity for change from within NATO. A French government of any party could be expected to resist moves towards a non-nuclear Europe and to offer to extend the French nuclear force to protect West Germany, a move which could be very disruptive within the West German Social Democrats. On the other hand, because France has withdrawn from the NATO military command structure, it lacks official weight within NATO.

Peace movements cannot rely too heavily on socialist parties coming to power, or on their willingness and ability to reject NATO reliance on nuclear weapons or to confront Washington. The likelihood of change depends partly on middle-ground political opinion supporting moves to alter NATO strategy and achieve greater independence from the US; an important shift in attitudes has taken place in the 1980s, but not enough to ensure wide support for unconditional measures of nuclear disarmament in Europe. Peace movements still have to influence public opinion, as well as holding out alternatives more radical than any government in the near future is likely to accept.

5 Jonathan Steele:
East–West and North–South

In a world where the activities of politicians are increasingly
defined by the mass media as the fittest subject for 'news', no
two events in the mid-1980s stood out more dramatically as
exceptions than the Ethiopian famine in 1984 and the
Chernobyl disaster in 1986. On the face of it, they differed
vastly from each other.

One was no 'event' at all, but the slow culmination of a
long-drawn-out ecological and climatic process, a tragedy
which had happened months before the outside world sat up
and took notice. It seemed to represent the failure of the
world's most primitive, 'low-tech' agriculture. The other was
a one-off catastrophe, a small though lethal blip on the hitherto almost totally clean screen of 'high-tech' nuclear industrial
achievement.

Yet, viewed from another perspective, Ethiopia and
Chernobyl had much in common. To many people they were
like two warning bells, sounding a note of doom which
transcended the normal categories of political debate. In one
case, the failure of millions of human beings to survive the
daily search for food exposed the inequity of economic
systems which can fund space travel but not sustain the
starving. In the second case, the huge area of contamination
created by the Chernobyl leak alerted many people for the
first time to the threat which nuclear technology poses to the
survival of the species. In the acutest possible way, Ethiopia
and Chernobyl highlighted the profound, existential questions which the peace movement and the campaigners for
development and justice in the Third World have long been
raising.

As millions of desperate women, children and men

stumbled out of the Ethiopian highlands and the Saharan dustbowl into relief camps in their own countries or abroad, and as the Chernobyl cloud spread across Europe, East and West, it was obvious that these were issues which surpassed national frontiers and ideological boundaries. To the famine, people responded with compassion and a scale of generosity which stunned the cynics. They greeted Chernobyl with alarm and anxiety. But both reactions were prompted by the sense that these were two unprecedented and colossal human disasters – 'the worst famine in the world' and 'the worst accident in the world'. The challenge for the peace and development movements is to build on this new public awareness before it fades totally. We must also demonstrate that solutions to them can no longer be kept separate.

In the past, those who argued for a new set of policies to deal with the Third World's crisis have tended to focus on two broad issues. One was how to deal with international economic problems – unequal terms of trade, protectionism in Western markets, massive indebtedness, and so on – which provoke and perpetuate social tensions in many developing countries. This is the classic interpretation of the 'North–South problem'. The other was how to find ways of controlling and reducing the arms trade.

Both issues have become more serious in recent years. The world's sudden discovery of Africa's catastrophic famine in 1984 led to the recognition that years of 'aid' had ended with a continent in total crisis. Measures had not been taken to protect land against erosion nor were stocks prepared as a reserve against bad weather. Basic food production had been ignored in favour of export crops and industrialization. Countries which followed the path of planting food for export saw the prices of these crops – whether sugar, cocoa, tea or coffee – decline. Efforts to stabilize their prices by intervening in the market with buffer stocks or export quotas did not work.

The road to development through industrialization worked for a few countries in Asia which were able to penetrate

Western markets for electronic goods and cheap clothing – though often the factories were Western-owned and the profits they made were also exported.

This was a path which only a few 'market leaders' could follow with success. The more that other countries tried to go down the same road, the greater the over-production and the downward pressure on prices, which led to protectionism in Western markets. At the same time, developing countries found themselves importing inflation from the North, as the prices of the machinery they needed in order to maintain their industrialization went up. Unilateral increases in interest rates by creditors on the debts incurred by developing nations on capital projects and imported technology created a mounting burden. The result was that in the early 1980s many Latin American countries were paying more money to the rich North than they were taking in. There was a reverse flow of 'aid' from the South to the North.

Meanwhile, the expansion of the arms trade continued, providing a further flow of cash from the South to the North. Between 1973 and 1982 military spending in the Third World is estimated to have gone up from US$44 bn to US$104 bn. The diversion of resources in already poor countries was immense. The Brandt Commission reported that just 5 per cent of the world's annual arms bill could finance a ten-year programme to pay for the developing countries' vital health and food needs. Increasing competition among the arms suppliers gave the Third World access to more and more advanced military technology. The new weapons have a growing power of destruction.

At the same time some countries, most notably Israel and Brazil, but also others in the Third World, have been developing their own armaments industries and becoming arms exporters. For some exporters, particularly those in Western Europe, the aim of the arms trade is primarily financial. They expect to be paid for the weapons they deliver and their primary customers, not surprisingly, are in the Middle East among the oil-producers who have the cash to pay. For other exporters such as Israel and particularly the two

superpowers, arms supplies have a primarily political purpose. They hope they can gain diplomatic, political or strategic influence with the arms recipients and are prepared, if
necessary, to give away their weapons.

The effect of this arms flow, whether as aid or trade, has
been catastrophic. Since 1945 the Third World has been the
cockpit for more than two hundred wars, and in almost every
case developed nations provided the weapons with which they
were fought. In many cases developed nations encouraged one
side or the other in its war aims. Cases where developed
nations sought to resolve conflicts have been few. The stark
historical record reveals one aspect of the connection between
war in the Third World and the policies of developed nations.

Western Europe has played a significant part in this arms
trade and in recent times its share has increased. Figures
prepared by the Congressional Research Service in the
United States showed that Western European nations ac-
counted for 31.3 per cent of all weapons sold under arms
agreements concluded in 1985.[1] This was higher than the
Soviet Union (30.4 per cent) and the United States (17.8 per
cent). For purposes of the survey Western Europe only
included the region's major arms exporters (Britain, France,
Italy and West Germany). Other Western European nations,
such as Belgium, Spain and Sweden, were counted separ-
ately, making Western Europe's real contribution to the
supply of the weapons of death even higher. Poverty in Third
World countries helps to breed war, and war of course breeds
poverty, and Western Europe is involved in both processes.

The depth of the crisis means that solving the North–
South problem and curbing the arms trade have become
immeasurably harder than they were a decade ago. Yet it
seems increasingly clear that dealing with either problem,
even if it could be tackled more successfully than hitherto, is
not enough. Nor is it sufficient to see the link between the
North and the South as primarily economic.

There is a more dangerous connection – what some have
called 'the deadly connection'. The spread of US–Soviet
competition in the Third World has led to the danger that

conventional wars which start in the Third World between allies or clients of the superpowers could be the spark which ignites a nuclear conflict between the superpowers themselves. How the link might be made in any future crisis is a matter for speculation. Analysts differ over the possible scenarios. But it is incontrovertible that the two occasions where the superpowers have come closest to nuclear war have been over Berlin in 1961 and Cuba in 1962 – fittingly, in terms of the 'deadly connection', one a crisis in Europe, the other in the Third World. More recently, the area of greatest danger has been the Middle East. After the U S-supported Israeli invasion of Lebanon, the constant pressure on Syria and the American attack on Libya, some would argue that the world cannot for ever rely on Soviet restraint to keep provocations by the United States and its allies against Moscow's friends from escalating to all-out confrontation.

The mechanism by which such a confrontation could occur is all too apparent. The growing economic crisis in most Third World countries, prompted by the debt burden and the inability to finance repayments or development by means of exports, is putting intolerable strain on societies. Many were already riven by severe inner tensions caused by extreme inequalities of income, problems of landlessness and exploitation, class and ethnic divisions, brutal government repression and other factors. In some countries these strains have already led to revolution. In others, revolution is barely being held back by authoritarian governments.

The United States and its Western European allies are deeply engaged at many levels. Firstly, their policies are helping to create and preserve the economic crisis. Secondly, in many cases they are supporting unpopular governments in trying to delay necessary reforms. Finally, once revolutions do occur, the West either fails to make the economic changes which would allow the new government to settle the old problems or, more frequently, it puts pressure on the new government and, in some cases, as with United States action over Nicaragua, attempts to overthrow it.

The process is fuelled by United States insistence on seeing every Third World country as an arena for East–West competition. The philosophy that he who is not with us is against us is superimposed on every problem, while the principle that countries may choose to be non-aligned receives short shrift. The initial post-war East–West confrontation in Europe was long ago extended globally. But the Reagan administration has raised it to a particularly sharp level. As long as superpower competition is seen as indivisible, leaving no part of the world free from its distorting effects, the connection between the armed truce which prevails precariously in Europe and the instability of the Third World is unbroken.

The fact that Europe's political climate is relatively stable by comparison with most of the Third World is not relevant here. East–West confrontation in Europe makes it easier to claim there is also an East–West confrontation in the Third World, and vice versa. By the same token, all efforts to break with Cold War thinking in Europe, escape from the psychosis of eternal vigilance towards an allegedly 'expanding' Soviet Union, re-evaluate the so-called Soviet threat to Western Europe, discuss radical new defence alternatives, and question the wisdom of Western Europe's link with the United States are vitiated as long as the independence of Third World countries is subverted.

How can Europe expect to get away from the political tensions and mutual suspicion which underpin the Warsaw Pact and NATO when the Reagan administration is permitted, virtually without challenge from its allies, to create new tensions against the sovereign government of Nicaragua in the name of a Western crusade against Communism? Europe, in short, cannot move towards a structure of peace in a vacuum.

Just as war preparation in Europe, and underdevelopment and East–West confrontation in the Third World are linked, so must peace and development be linked. There can be no solution in Europe without a solution in the Third World. Both must proceed together. It is vital, therefore, for the peace movement and for Third World liberation movements to work hand in hand. They are not engaged on separate agendas, but on a common agenda, even though different groups may put their energies into different items on it.

Within this common agenda, two broad strategies can be defined. One is to introduce a wholly new set of alternative economic policies for the Third World, based on a non-exploitative relationship with the developed countries. In this way some of the underlying social problems of Third World countries could be alleviated and solved. The other strategy is to end the East–West confrontation in Europe, and thereby reduce and end it in the Third World also. This has become the overriding political question now.

Activists for peace and activists for development have for too long tended to be separated in the First World, as though they were campaigning on unconnected issues. For some it was a failure, or an unwillingness, to acknowledge connections. Others felt there was a contradiction between the pressures in many Third World situations to support the armed struggle of a liberation movement and the more pacific tendencies of the disarmament movement in Europe. At one extreme many 'Third Worldists' indulge in a kind of escapism, preferring to engage themselves in apparently remote issues rather than confront pressing problems at home. Or they act from paternalistic/maternalistic motives of charity, giving money to the beggar without asking why the beggar is there. In contrast to this spurious altruism, the peace movement has been accused of being excessively selfish, worrying about the future survival of the North rather than the present misery of the South. As one Third World writer has put it, 'the disarmament movement in Europe and the United States is, by and large, a-historical, technocentric, nuko-centric, ethnocentric, and phobo-centric. It is so obsessed with the technology of war, specifically nuclear war, that it ignores the causes of it.'[2]

Living in countries allied to the major superpower, the peace and development movements in Britain and those Western European nations which belong to NATO have a primary responsibility. Their first objective must be to limit NATO's involvement to Europe and North America, and prevent any further weakening in NATO's original confinement of its sphere of operations to those areas.

The second objective must be to restrain the US from seeing threats to its vital interests where none exist, from interpreting every local crisis either as a move in an East-versus-West game or as a challenge to American virility, and from intervening abroad with force or the threat of force.

The third objective must be to support and strengthen the concept of non-alignment among Third World nations. Paying lip-service to the concept of independence has to be supplemented by concrete moves to make genuine independence possible. Measures could include a ban on foreign bases, or the establishment of 'zones of non-intervention' from which foreign ships, aircraft and military facilities would be banned.

These last two objectives presuppose a much greater willingness than European NATO member-states have yet shown to criticize and distance themselves from the United States. They assume that the NATO alliance itself will become a much looser structure in which sovereign members exercise the right of debate and dissent rather than being forced into an artificial unity. They also assume that the alliance will have to move in a non-nuclear direction towards a policy of no first use of nuclear weapons, and ultimately of reliance on conventional weapons alone.

At the moment the United States is able to operate a kind of nuclear blackmail on its allies by threatening to withdraw the 'strategic nuclear umbrella' which is the mainstay of current NATO strategy in Europe. Any signs of European independence can be countered by the implicit or explicit threat that the United States will not defend Europe unless Europe is prepared to share more in its own defence. As long as NATO strategy relies on US nuclear weapons, this threat will persist.

A move towards a NATO based on conventional weapons would not only increase European security by reducing the risk of nuclear war but also permit a looser and more open framework for decision-making. It would be a step on the road towards the dismantling of both military blocs in Europe. Ultimately the loosening of NATO will help to bring about what should be the fourth objective of Western European nations – the restoration of the non-alignment of Europe, East and West.

Let us take these four objectives in turn.

1. Blocking NATO's 'Out-of-area' Activities

Hints from NATO leaders of the need for the alliance to take an interest in 'out-of-area' problems began with the oil crisis of 1973.

Oil was described as a strategic commodity, and any interruption in its supply was considered as a threat to the West – and in 'the West' NATO leaders increasingly included Japan. The first hint of direct United States military action to seize the oil fields if the Arab and Gulf states tried to repeat their 1973 embargo came from Henry Kissinger in 1975. It prompted a warning from President Sadat of Egypt that the Arab oil producers would blow up the wells rather than permit their capture.

Early in 1977 the Carter administration started planning for a mobile US intervention force to act in non-NATO emergencies. This evolved two years later into what became known as the Rapid Deployment Force. A central command was created over a number of US units which could be drawn on when needed, and plans were made to dispatch a fleet of 'maritime pre-positioning ships' stuffed with arms and ammunition to the Indian Ocean. The ships would be on permanent standby, while overflying and refuelling rights and communications facilities would be sought in friendly countries for planes which would airlift troops.

Oil was seen as the link which could bring the United States, Western Europe and Japan together, providing both an economic and a geographic 'common interest'.

President Carter's National Security Adviser, Zbigniew

Brzezinski, announced that the White House considered the Middle East to be as important strategically to the United States as Western Europe and the Far East, and considered that a 'threat to the security of any one is an automatic threat to the security of the other two'.[3]

Throwing this new web of 'common interest and security' over Western Europe, the Middle East and east Asia posed problems of jurisdiction for NATO, which increased when the Reagan administration took office in January 1981 and soon embarked on a policy of active intervention in the Third World. The Pentagon saw parts of NATO, particularly the Mediterranean member nations, as playing a dual role. No longer were they there ostensibly to help the United States in the defence of Europe. They were also linked to the Rapid Deployment Force's operations in the Mediterranean, north Africa and the Middle East.

In 1983 the Italian government gave its official blessing to the RDF. The United States military base at Sigonella in Sicily, which had been a support base and nuclear-weapons store for the US Sixth Fleet, was upgraded and plans were made to expand military facilities on the island for 15,000 men.

In Spain the bilateral treaty with the United States gave Washington new points of logistical support, storage and refuelling for aircraft of the RDF. In 1981 the Reagan administration persuaded the right-wing government of Leopoldo Calvo Sotelo to bring Spain into NATO, and tie the country more closely to American planning and infrastructure arrangements for the Mediterranean.

Taking for granted a community of interest between Western Europe and itself, the Reagan administration began to talk of a 'division of labour' in global security. By this it was meant that Europe should provide more conventional forces for NATO, to allow the United States, in particular contingencies, to use some of its 300,000 troops based in West Germany for 'out-of-area' purposes. During the Lebanese crisis in 1983 it persuaded Britain, France and Italy to supply troops for a US-dominated multinational force in Beirut. The effect was to blur the lines between NATO's traditional area of operations and the rest of the world.

The process reached a new highwater mark in April 1986 when the Reagan administration made its night-time bombing raids on Tripoli and other Libyan cities. Using F-111 bombers based in Britain, which most people had imagined to be assigned exclusively to NATO, the United States struck at an independent Mediterranean country. The pretext that the Libyan government was involved in promoting terrorism against American targets was at best flimsy, since no proof was produced by independent sources. The degree of American retaliation, even if such proof were available, was out of all proportion. The hypocrisy and use of double standards was staggering, since the United States was itself involved in terrorism against the governments of Nicaragua and Angola. When the International Court of Justice, three months after the Libyan raids, found the Reagan administration guilty of supporting terrorism against Nicaragua, no one suggested that the Sandinistas would have been right to launch a bombing raid on Washington.

A number of Western European governments – France, Italy, and Spain – refused the United States the right to send its planes across their territory to Libya. This was a vital gesture of non-participation, which must be built upon.

The Reagan administration showed no sign of accepting it. At a NATO maritime strategy conference two months later, the US Defense Secretary Caspar Weinberger called for NATO to expand its naval operations to the Pacific, the Indian Ocean and the Gulf. 'We must have leverage for action in corners of the globe far removed from the north Atlantic, places where developments can mightily affect NATO's security,' he said.[4] The United States has been trying to persuade its allies to support its global interventions under three headings: 'compensation, facilitation and participation'. 'Compensation' means providing European troops to fill gaps left by absent US troops. 'Facilitation' means providing bases and other assistance for US troops moving into operations outside Europe. 'Participation' would require Western European governments to take part in US military adventures.

2. Restraining the United States

In the late 1970s, as described in the previous section, the United States started on a new policy of global interventionism. After the end of the Vietnam war and the collapse of US covert intervention in Angola in 1975, there was a brief period when the United States withdrew from direct military operations in the Third World. But, as Michael Klare has put it, a new war soon began – 'not a war with guns and bullets, but a war with words, the war to reverse the "Vietnam syndrome"'.[5] The 'Vietnam syndrome' was the American public's disinclination to engage in further military interventions in internal Third World conflicts. To many decision-makers the syndrome was an unacceptable restraint on the White House's freedom of action. For a time the Carter administration accepted this restraint, at least in areas not connected with the main sources of the world's oil. It acquiesced, for example, in the overthrow of the Nicaraguan dictator, Anastasio Somoza, in July 1979.

With Carter's defeat in November 1980, the struggle to overturn the 'Vietnam syndrome' moved into a more determined phase. The Reagan administration systematically went about removing the various constraints on presidential action passed by the United States Congress, and restored the covert action departments of the Central Intelligence Agency to their former strength.

The administration put together a group of former National Guard officers from the Somoza dictatorship, and gave them enough arms and finance through indirect channels to form a paramilitary force which aimed to subvert the new government of Nicaragua. It gave money to rebel movements in Angola and Kampuchea, and to the resistance groups operating from Pakistan against the Soviet occupation forces in Afghanistan. It vastly increased the amount of US military aid to El Salvador and discouraged the Salvadorean government's tentative acceptance of peace talks with the guerrilla movements. In 1983 it took advantage of a power struggle within the leadership of the government of Grenada, and invaded the tiny Caribbean island. It conducted a powerful propaganda campaign to convince the American public that virtually every sign of turbulence in the Third World was caused or provoked by the Soviet Union or its close allies. In 1986 it exaggerated the issue of terrorism to find a cover for military action against Libya and new pressure on Syria.

In fact the only unilateral Third World intervention made by the Soviet Union – albeit a massive one – was its invasion of Afghanistan in December 1979. The invasion did not profoundly alter the regional geo-political situation, and there were grounds for seeing it as the result of special circumstances. Afghanistan shared a border with the Soviet Union and for twenty years before 1979 already had closer political and economic links with the Soviet Union than with any other developed country.

There was no evidence at the time of the invasion, or in the years which followed, that the Soviet Union intended the move into Afghanistan to be a springboard for further advances in south Asia. It was a desperate and illegal move to prop up a collapsing regime. Soviet military theory, matched by Soviet deployments, assumes that East–West conflicts will rapidly escalate to full-scale war. The vast majority of Soviet divisions are geared for a full-scale engagement with the West in Europe, or with China on the Sino-Soviet border. The Red Army does not have the same separation between 'heavy' divisions for European crises and 'light' divisions for Third World crises as does the United States. Most Soviet forces are committed to strategic defence.

Nevertheless during the late 1970s the Soviet Union heightened its willingness and ability to give military support to radical Third World governments which asked for its aid. It increased its arms deliveries to a range of Arab states. These moves were prompted by a number of factors. A series of Third World revolutions, from Angola and Mozambique to Grenada and Nicaragua, gave Moscow a range of radical states which looked to it for aid in the face of internal or external threats.

The more the United States sought to manipulate internal rebel movements or create external pressure against radical Third World governments, the more the Soviet Union was invited by these governments to respond. In the Middle East, the expansionist thrust of Israel's policy, expressed most dramatically in the invasion of the Lebanon in 1982 and the settlement policy on the West Bank of the Jordan, made it almost inevitable that the Soviet Union would become more closely linked with Syria. The more the United States insisted on seeing the Soviet Union as the global challenger, the stronger was the pressure and the temptation for the Soviet Union to take up the challenge. As the self-appointed standard-bearer of a new socialist model for humankind, the Soviet Union increasingly began to take action in the Third World in support of its revolutionary rhetoric, although always, of course, making sure that Soviet interests remained paramount.

In practice, Soviet actions remained cautious, given the enormous imbalance between American global power and that of the Soviet Union. But the potential for a U S–Soviet clash has grown and the primary onus of responsibility is on the United States to avoid it.

Its European allies should play a role in restraining the United States. They should persuade the United States not to view every Third World crisis as a threat to itself. They should point to the historical traditions, the social inequalities, the economic burdens, and the lack of space for independent action which create tension and prompt revolutions that have nothing to do with the Soviet Union. They should argue the case that global stability is best served by supporting the non-alignment of Third World states rather than by drawing them into alliance with one of the superpowers. They should loosen the exploitative economic links which tie the Third World to the First and help to provoke internal crises.

Above all, they should assert these points publicly. A quiet distancing of allied governments from Washington's policy towards Nicaragua and Libya has only limited value and little chance of influencing the public debate in the United States Congress and the American media. Throughout 1985 and 1986 the Reagan administration was able to whittle down Congressional resistance to open funding of the Nicaraguan contras by constant appeals to American patriotism and the alleged need to stand up with freedom-fighters against a Soviet-backed dictatorship. The Congressional opposition allowed itself to be driven into criticizing the President mainly from a position of pragmatic politics rather than from one of principle. Would funding the contras push the Sandinistas into the arms of Moscow? Would economic pressure be a better tactic? Would it suck the United States into a war in which American boys would eventually lose their lives?

Only a few Congressmen were willing to raise the fundamental issue that the United States had no right to intervene against Nicaragua, whatever its form of government. Even when the International Court of Justice in The Hague, the world's highest international legal body, ruled that the United States was acting in breach of international law, this had little effect in the United States. If Western European governments had emphasized this point themselves throughout the long Congressional debate they might have had some impact. Even when the contras kidnapped twelve West German citizens and held them hostage for almost a month in 1986, the West German government was very subdued in appealing to the United States government for help in securing their release. To their credit, no Western European government went along with the US trade embargo on Nicaragua, but, again, they did not advertise their non-compliance with American policy. The result was that the US Congress had no real sense that the Reagan administration was considered by its allies to be acting illegally. Worse than that, the administration was able to suggest to Congress that its European allies were not going along with US policy against Nicaragua and its Soviet backers only out of their traditional weakness in taking a stand on matters of ideological principle – in other words, a kind of appeasement. (Of course the administration was right – except that the person the Western European governments were weakly appeasing was President Reagan.)

A similar pattern was followed in the case of the US campaign against Libya – some mild distancing from US action, hints that force was not the best way to handle the issue, but no public challenge to legitimacy of US actions. Again, the administration argued that it was only cowardice in the face of terrorism (Gadafy's) that had prevented Europe from supporting the United States.

3. *Supporting Third World Non-alignment*

One reason for the propensity of the United States, and to a lesser extent of the Soviet Union, to see the Third World as a stage for playing out their global competition is the economic weakness and political instability of Third World states. Third World states would be able to assert their own independence more effectively if they were stronger. The best way to support Third World non-alignment is therefore to encourage economic development and the promotion of social justice in African, Asian and Latin American nations.

This is not the place to go into detail on the various measures which have been proposed elsewhere for bringing prosperity to the Third World. They include numerous options from re-orientating agriculture towards food for local consumption to cancelling the debts incurred in the 1970s.

A second set of suggested measures would bring about international controls on the arms trade. There is already international agreement on the non-proliferation of nuclear weapons and nuclear arms technology, though it has been breached many times and is not accepted by many states. This should be extended to a curb on the proliferation of conventional weapons. Britain, France, West Germany and Italy are major exporters.

A third priority is to provide a new international basis for conflict resolution. This, clearly, is a task of enormous difficulty, when one considers the relative failure of the United Nations. At the least a start could be made on creating zones of superpower non-intervention, in which US and Soviet ships, manoeuvres, aircraft and foreign bases would be banned. The waters of the Mediterranean and the Caribbean, for example, could be de-militarized and put off-limits to superpower navies. The Persian Gulf and the Indian Ocean could also be made zones of non-intervention. A code of conduct for the two superpowers in Third World conflicts might be negotiated through the United Nations. An attempt could be made to outlaw foreign military assistance to rebel groups within Third World countries, unless a three-to-one majority in the UN General Assembly agreed. This could make aid to the African National Congress and SWAPO more easily available, while restricting aid to UNITA in Angola or the MNR in Mozambique, on the grounds that the ANC have widespread international support and legitimacy while the other two movements do not.

Western Europe, where Britain and France are still major naval powers, could play a significant part in promoting zones of non-intervention by renouncing its own plans to operate in these areas.

States which have made a conspicuous effort to remain or become non-aligned ought to be supported politically and diplomatically by Western European governments on the grounds that they are showing the way forward. Nicaragua, Mozambique and New Zealand are countries which, in the mid-1980s, tried hard to remain non-aligned or put conditions on their membership of an alliance. Britain ought to have given them strong political support, by dispatching observers to the Nicaraguan elections, for example, or publicly praising the New Zealand Prime Minister's call for a ban on visits by nuclear warships. South African threats to Mozambique should have been firmly denounced and punished. The Spanish government's decision to hold a referendum in 1986 on whether to remain a member of NATO should have been welcomed in Western Europe, and other

NATO members should not have encouraged Spain to stay in. No country in Europe, with the exception of Portugal, is further from the Soviet Union, and nothing had changed in the balance of forces to justify from a military point of view the entry of a new member. The only foreign pressure for Spain to join was political, and it came almost exclusively from the United States. The United States, which had happily lived with the Franco dictatorship, suddenly argued that to bring Spain in NATO would strengthen democracy by giving the Spanish top brass a stake in staying in a democratic club. The real US interest, however, was in Spain's position in the Mediterranean.

The Spanish referendum was a good opportunity for Europeans to take a stand in favour of the principle of a loosening of the blocs by resisting the enlargement of one of them and the strengthening of its growing potential for Mediterranean, anti-Arab intervention. Western Europeans approved the efforts which Romania made in the 1960s to find a special status within the Warsaw Pact, and they would no doubt disapprove if Yugoslavia were to join the Warsaw Pact. Spanish resistance to NATO was a similar test case and it was unfortunate that the referendum in Spain was manipulated by a one-sided media campaign which equated NATO either with the Common Market or with 'Europe' (undefined), without many Europeans outside Spain pointing out the fallacy of the argument. There were other factors behind the Spanish government's success. The Prime Minister, Felipe Gonzalez, turned the referendum into a vote on his government's total performance, and promised that Spain would remain non-nuclear. But if more West Europeans had rejected the argument that NATO needed Spain, more Spaniards might have rejected the argument that Spain needed NATO. As it was, a vote for NATO was seen as a vote for internationalism and a vote against the isolation to which the long years of the Franco dictatorship had condemned the country.

4. Restoring European Non-alignment

The three previous sections have discussed ways in which countries can work towards a strengthening non-alignment while remaining within NATO. The Spanish referendum showed how hard the road ahead is, and how deeply embedded the forces still are which favour the maintenance of two opposed blocks in Europe. Ultimately the best way to reduce the risk of a superpower clash in the Third World is to move towards the de-alignment of Europe. Just as the Nuclear Non-proliferation Treaty has been weakened by continued French and British insistence on maintaining nuclear weapons, so it is difficult to press for the removal of superpower competition in the Third World as long as Europe remains the deployment ground for the largest East–West arsenals in the world.

The defenders of the status quo in Europe frequently claim that the existence of nuclear weapons there has guaranteed 'forty years of peace'. They point, almost with satisfaction, to the two hundred conventional wars in the Third World since 1945 as proof that where there is no nuclear stand-off there is bound to be war.

The argument is dangerously complacent, first because of the role which the superpowers and their European allies have played in fuelling conflict in the Third World, but also because of the numerous occasions on which nuclear weapons have almost been detonated in Third World conflicts by one of the superpowers, with the risk that this could have ignited a conflagration in which Europe would not have been spared.

Barry Blechman and Stephen Kaplan[6] of the Brookings Institution in Washington have identified nineteen occasions between 1945 and 1973 when the United States put nuclear forces on the alert, and made plans for their use. Twelve of them were in the Third World (Uruguay, 1947; Korea, 1950, 1953, 1968; Guatemala, 1954; China, 1954, 1958; Middle East, 1956, 1958 twice, 1973; Cuba, 1962). Since then another incident involving US nuclear weapons over Vietnam has been disclosed. The fact that there have been no further incidents since 1973 is probably due to the Soviet Union's emergence as the nuclear equal of the United States after a decade of sharply building up its forces. But it is not a cause for relief. The sense of underlying tension between the superpowers in the Third World is greater now than ever. The Reagan administration is unwilling to accept a Soviet position of influence in the Third World and has started to try to roll it back in the few countries where the Soviet Union is the dominant superpower.

A lasting solution can only be found if *both* superpowers' positions of influence are rolled back. This cannot be done by each superpower confronting and hoping to remove the other, but by Third World countries ensuring that both are rejected. Western Europe could have a major role in this process, once a majority current in public opinion accepts that peace in the world depends on a reduction of superpower pressures, and the enlargement of the freedom of manoeuvre of smaller nations.

At the same time, the spread of nuclear weapons in the Third World must be prevented. Regardless of the superpower confrontation, there is an increasing danger of a nuclear clash between Third World nations themselves, now that at least six states possess nuclear weapons of their own. The Chernobyl disaster showed how pervasive radiation can be, and how far it can spread. Even a 'small-scale' nuclear clash between Third World countries would kill tens of thousands of people in the area immediately and could pose major risks to Europe. The idea that Europe is a kind of sanctuary, immune from nuclear danger, is a myth.

There can be no real peace in Europe until the political division in the heart of the continent is healed. A goal for the departure of all foreign forces in Europe must be set. The Mediterranean should become a 'zone of superpower non-intervention', starting with the banning of all U S and Soviet naval deployments. The southern European sections of the two alliances should be dropped, with Bulgaria and Romania leaving the Warsaw Pact, and Greece, Turkey, Spain and Portugal leaving NATO, so that the pacts thereafter only cover the central front. This would be an interim stage towards the total dissolution of both.

The Western peace movement and the various movements for social justice and independence in the Third World must join hands. The driving force behind the First World's exploitative relationship with the Third World is not just a desire for raw materials and markets for their own sake. It is also a desire to deny them to the Soviet Union. This 'strategy of denial' reinforces the West's search for hegemonic control over the entire developing world.

Historians are divided over how far the American strategic planners, who maintained the victorious United States' capacity for global intervention and policing after the Second World War, really felt the Soviet Union was a threat.

Did they wish to create a system of open trading and unimpeded access for American capital for reasons of ideology and perceived national interest, and was the 'Soviet threat' used artificially to overcome isolationist tendencies in the United States? Would they, according to this theory, have followed the same economic and military policies even if the Soviet Union did not exist? Or did they feel that the Soviet Union was an expansionist power which had to be contained at all costs, and was it this drive for containment which led the United States increasingly into a long-term global military role?

In understanding and reacting to the present danger, there is no need to agree on the origins of the post-1945 American posture. By now the two impulses have become blurred and the reality forty years later is a complex mixture of both attitudes. The ideology of containment is deeply embedded in the desire to maintain hegemony over all the territory once dominated by the European imperial powers. The battleground is not only the Third World, but Europe too. United States policy imposes a false need for unity on Western Europe, symbolized by the overworked metaphor according to which the Soviet Union is constantly alleged to be trying to 'drive a wedge' into Western Europe or between Western Europe and the USA. Independent Western European action is discouraged because it 'weakens alliance cohesion' or 'sends the wrong signal'. Independent American action is, of course, acceptable.

Any strengthening of the military link between US European and US global policy must be rejected. But the link exists at more than just the military level. Both aspects of US policy form part of a single ideological and political web. Western Europeans cannot realistically expect to repudiate one aspect of US policy and not the other. We must work towards a new system of non-alignment and non-confrontation with the East.

The development movement, for its part, must try to create the political conditions within Western Europe for a non-exploitative relationship with the Third World. Aid that is used to support 'pro-Western' regimes is misconceived, as is aid which strengthens repressive regimes. The debt burden must be written off and fair terms of trade introduced.

Above all, the peace and development movements will have to see that their goals are united. The campaign for a peace settlement in Europe and the campaign for economic justice and political independence in the Third World cannot be separated. Each is unattainable without the other.

Notes

1. *The New York Times*, May 14, 1986.
2. Eqbal Ahmad in *END Journal*, April/May 1985, pp. 14, 18.
3. *Chicago Sun-Times*, 20 December 1979.
4. *Observer*, 15 June 1986.
5. M. T. Klare, *Beyond the 'Vietnam Syndrome'*, Washington, DC, Institute for Policy Studies, 1981, p. 1.
6. B. M. Blechman and S. S. Kaplan, *Force without War*, Washington, DC, Brookings Institution, 1978, p. 48.

PART THREE

Rethinking Europe

6   Caesar Voûte: Whose Europe?
A View from the West

Standing water ... breeds reptiles of the mind.
William Blake

If you want to sort out the problems of Europe you must first
deal with The Bomb. That is straightforward. The nuclear
threat has united all Europeans. Our incredible diversity,
our dozens of languages, our century upon century of bloody
and usually mindless tribal conflicts – the Transylvanian
question and who owns the cod which swim around Iceland
– all are so much drivel in the face of The Bomb.

The Bomb has abolished East and West. The Bomb
commands us all to love one another. When it is abolished,
Czech typewriters will type Dutch, Dutch typewriters will
type Czech, and English typewriters will type both. Let the
floods clap their hands, let the hills be joyful together, as the
people of Europe, hand-in-hand, proceed to Ban the Bomb,
for radiation needs no passport. And then, like the parting of
the waters of the Red Sea, the American and Russian
armies will withdraw from Europe, and the people from East
and West will meet in the middle and fall into each others'
arms.

All right, this is a caricature. But this mood was stirring
amongst millions of us when we met in those amazing demonstrations in the capitals of Western Europe in 1981, and
again in 1983, and when Greenham Common became a European symbol of resistance. And in the internationalist peace
organizations we saw the opportunities open up, when the
dialogue with Charter 77 began and the independent peace
groups in Hungary and the GDR and the Moscow Trust
Group emerged. It was all coming together, we had cracked
it. The system of the blocs had been completely undermined

and its collapse was imminent. You could not help getting caught up in that mood.

And yet there was always something niggling in the background. It was all a bit too straightforward. Europe isn't like that. Things are supposed to be complicated in Europe. Something as stupid as The Bomb cannot be the generator of inspired visions for Europe. If you argue everything back to The Bomb you end up like Cousin Amos preaching to the congregation of the Quivering Brethren apropos of hell:

'Ye know, doan't ye, what it feels like when ye burn yer hand in takin' a cake out of the oven or wi' a match when ye're lightin' one of they godless cigarettes? Aye, it stings wi' a fearful pain, doan't it? And ye run away to clap a bit o' butter on it to take the pain away. Ah, but (an impressive pause) *there'll be no butter in hell* . . .! Yer whoal body will be burnin' and stingin' wi' that unbearable pain, and yer blackened tongues will be stickin' out of yer mouth, and yer cracked lips will try to scream out for a drop of water, but no sound woan't come because yer throat is drier than the sandy desert and yer eyes will be beatin' like great red-hot balls against yer shrivelled eyelids . . .'[1]

The Quivering Brethren loved it, and Cousin Amos's imagination was so inflamed by people's likely confinement to the boilerhouse in their afterlife that he never got round to discussing in his sermons what any alternative might be like.

Nuclear weapons *are* of course exceedingly dangerous and strategies of nuclear posturing are a total perversion of any concept of relations between peoples. The campaign against all this is an unconditional priority. But in such a bleak campaigning context it is very difficult to form a vision of what you are campaigning *for*. There are good practical reasons why this amazing movement of peace activists which has been taking shape all around us cannot itself form a blueprint of what Europe could be. But they are an absolutely essential part of a much larger political, social and cultural laboratory where ideas, dreams and visions for Europe are put to the test of real people.

First I want to stay with the idea of laboratory, for it has been expanding a great deal. It grows like chickweed and has even been taking root in a few places where it wasn't really wanted. I will start with a glimpse in the very core of NATO war planning for Europe.

I have here some documents in Dutch – and in one case in a mixture of Dutch and English – which were definitely never meant to be public. They are internal fictitious 'scenarios' for the biannual NATO-wide exercises WINTEX/ CIMEX for 1981 and 1983. These are command-level exercises, military and civilian structures combined, which take place mainly on paper. They rehearse the start of the Third World War, from 'increasing international tension' up to nuclear war. The command and organizational structures are tested and to make the whole thing more realistic the participants are given all sorts of *ad hoc* problems to cope with.

NATO HQ supplies an overall political scenario and lists of typical 'incidents'.[2] Participating organizations in each country (army staffs, government ministers, local government in some cases, the railways, postal service and telecommunications, and so on) are provided with the NATO scenario and with details of national events and incidents, and they then add further details themselves. The scenarios I have at hand happen to be those of the Dutch PTT, i.e. the equivalent of what used to be the GPO in the UK.[3] These are intriguing – though hideous – documents. It is thought-provoking to see how the sections dealing with local events in Holland have introduced the peace movement as a source of problems and incidents to be coped with in the transition to war. It would be tedious to go through it all entry by entry, but you can trace how between 1981 and 1983 the war planners have been trying to figure out what the peace movement is really about. The later version shows a decrease in pro-'Orange' (that's Russia) protests and propaganda, and there is much more 'non-aligned' protest by people in 1983. To a limited extent, even the war planners themselves felt the need to join the laboratory.

But ultimately (in these scenarios) they got hold of entirely the wrong end of the stick. The last entry in the 1983 scenario reads:

2 March 1983 at start of duty period
Supporters of the action group 'Europe for the Europeans' hold large demonstrations in Amsterdam and Rotterdam directed against the arrival of American troops. At the railway shunting yard De Rietlanden, in Amsterdam, fourteen closed railway trucks are set fire to and are destroyed by demonstrators.

I am not interested in the insinuated violence just now. 'Europe for the Europeans', is that what we are about? Recently a few people from the British peace movement visited Poland to meet various prominent people in Solidarnosc. They reported back that they suggested the slogan, 'Europe for the Europeans', and it went down well. But here we have something which must be examined with great care. This slogan turns out to have a very sordid history.

In May 1940 a German industrialist, Werner Daitz, was running a kind of economic think-tank for the Nazi leadership. He submitted a memorandum outlining a kind of EEC structure for an economic community of all the lands Germany was going to conquer, and in this memorandum he coined the slogan 'Europe to the Europeans'. The slogan was picked up and widely used for Nazi propaganda purposes.[4] (I am not, of course, for one moment suggesting that there are Fascist sympathies in Solidarnosc.)

Let's have a closer look at the mentality of the people who compile scenarios for transition to war and who in this context can just about envisage a pan-European peace movement. What is supposed to happen to immigrant communities (now the second and third generations after the arrival of the guest workers)?

We find in the entries for the anticipated crisis that they would want to leave the country in droves. It is assumed that they constitute a profound nuisance at the railway stations, which can't cope with the extra traffic and disruption anyway. It is assumed that they would engage in rioting and vandalism at airports. *And it is assumed that contagious diseases will break out amongst them as they are congregating at the railway stations.*[5]

It is generally assumed that large numbers of people would be on the move all over the place, soldiers, refugees from Germany, and so on. But only these, mainly Mediterranean and north African, people are supposed to be carriers of such diseases, even though they have been receiving exactly the same health care as the rest of the population. A deeply racist assumption was made here by the people who could just about envisage a 'protest and survive' type movement under the motto 'Europe for the Europeans'.

But our chickweed laboratory has also been growing into more public regions of N A T O. What about this, in *NATO Review*?

Mistrust and hatred between peoples, nations and systems are the causes of conflicts and fears of war, not soldiers with their weapons. Thus only a reduction of hate and the creation of well-founded confidence will in the long run result in true peace. We need hate-free zones in Europe . . .

This was written by Alois Mertes of the West German Foreign Affairs Ministry in the February 1985 issue.[6] Mertes has not yet cottoned on to the fact that soldiers with their weapons have a vested interest in *inducing* mistrust and hatred. Nevertheless, this kind of language does show evidence of influence by the European peace movements. He has thought about the idea of nuclear-free zones and he has come up with a wider notion which sounds more positive. Not one of protest, but one of peace-building: hate-free zones.

Now I must admit that I have taken the quotation a little out of context, but Mertes isn't so innocent either, for a little further on he gave his game away:

. . . an age-old longing for harmony, non-violence and justice between states, deeply rooted in human nature.

Between *states*, not between communities and people, or nations. But whereas the anonymous compilers of transition-to-war exercise scenarios got firmly hold of the wrong end of the stick, Mertes, with a little encouragement and perseverence, might *find* the stick and begin to compare the two ends.

I have been rooting around for some buzz words, some signposts for my theme: 'Europe for the Europeans'; 'hate-free zones'. I am now ready to go into the laboratory myself. There is going to be a lot of general clutter on my bench, but all the time one central idea is bubbling on the fire. It is another buzz word, one I spotted in a peace movement publication this time. It is the notion of 'infrastructure of peace'.

To be a European now is to go through life with an acute sense that something is missing, has been cut off from us. It is the exasperating feeling that there is a European experience which is very close to us, and yet as inaccessible as ways of life on one of the outer planets. And what makes it even more maddening is that any attempted description of this European experience is going to be a falsification. You can't get at the *wholeness* of it.

I can only make hints. Here is something from my own country. In the fifties and sixties we were getting those big Wurlitzer jukeboxes in pubs and so on. They were of course loaded up with the latest hits from the English-speaking world, but also with indigenous popular music. One of the home-produced hits was called 'Amsterdam Weeps', sung by a singer called Rika Jansen. The song was a lament – with incantation-like recitatives between the verses – about the disappeared Jewish life and the lost Jewish communities of the city.

Now Rika Jansen made her name (and presumably a fortune) in a form of popular music which is, as far as I know, unique to Holland: the *smartlap* (literally: 'sorrow cloth'). The subject matter is always people's misfortune in one way or another and someone's (usually a close relative's) response to the inevitable tragic fate. 'Oh father dear, please drink no more . . .' type stuff.

The songs are typically sung as duets, on a diminished third throughout, and the dramatic effect is heightened by

leaps and glissandos in the singing, maybe traces of something Spanish or oriental in the genre's origins. In terms of
lyrics and music the genre is utter and total kitsch. But
imagine trash like this taken to its logical conclusion. That is
exactly what the genre has done. It is so over the top that it
is impossible to make a parody. Any such attempt ends up
being taken for the real thing. The genre is *its own* parody.

But infants do die, fathers do ruin their families through
alcoholism in real life, and there is a haunting irony in these
songs. They are hilarious and they stir genuine emotion at
the same time. The response is like looking at those gimmicky
metallic picture postcards or pictures on ribbed plastic, where
the slightest movement changes the entire picture because
the reflection of the light has changed.

I am explaining at length because I find it so extraordinary
that Rika Jansen got away with it. To lament the loss of a
community and way of life, through calculated mass murder,
using this bizarre genre of working-class pop music was the
cultural equivalent of tightrope walking. One wrong word,
perhaps one wrong phrase in the music, and it would have
been a blasphemy.

The song was popular for a long time: you might still hear
it on the radio now and then. I am trying to say that this
feeling of bereavement, of loss, when part of our cultural and
social diversity has gone (or if access to it is lost) is one which
not only intellectuals or culturally sophisticated people experience.

There are other pointers to this feeling of being culturally
somehow incomplete which we Europeans seem to have. I
am amazed by so many people's obsessive interest in the
history of their local surroundings. Slide-shows of 'Lowestoft
as it used to be' fill large local halls to the rafters, again and
again; the demand is never exhausted. And I am convinced
this is a Europe-wide phenomenon. In 1982 I happened to
come across a few issues of the *Neue Banater Zeitung*, the
German-language local rag of Temisoara in the Banat of
Temesvár, a region of Europe where people speak German,
Hungarian or Romanian, any two, or all three languages.

The size of this daily and the quality of its paper indicate that Romania has a desperate shortage of newsprint, and every newspaper is under strict control by Ceauşescu's ruling clique. But even in this exotic and strictly controlled version of the *East Anglian Daily Times*, nostalgic columns are filled with local reminiscences going back to the days of the Habsburg Empire.[7]

I want to give one more example, directly out of the European peace movement. In November 1984 young people, mainly from peace groups in Italy, Yugoslavia and Austria, met at an informal peace camp in the Slovenian village of Srednji Vrh, which is situated at the point where the three countries meet. I will have more to say about the event, but now I want to highlight a little incidental remark by one of the participants from this region when he reported the event in an Austrian little journal:

> ... While my grandfather, for example, would have been able to make himself understood in the various languages [i.e. German, Slovene and Italian], I myself was glad that the 'official' language at the event was English.[8]

Again a consciousness, by a young peacenik this time, of having lost direct contact with Europe's diversity, and that in the very region in which he lives. The destructive force was that of state nationalisms. Those regions where different peoples lived side by side, mixed and met, were regions of exchange. Places where *European* culture was made through the wondrous ways we can transmit poetry, stories, ideas and ideals across languages and local ways of life.

Benedict Anderson, in an important recent study,[9] has analysed in the most thoughtful way how nationalism has made such borderlands into peripheral regions in modern times. These themes are also worked through by the great German writers Günther Grass from West Germany and Johannes Bobrowski from the GDR, in their stories of the German–Polish and German–Lithuanian borderlands. They search for answers to the questions of what went wrong, what mistakes were made, what opportunities were lost? And is it not extraordinary that their stories have achieved a degree of popularity even in insular Britain?

There is a mood about in Europe that we have lost the very thing which made us Europeans: the creative tension of living our own language and culture mixed up with day-to-day contact with, or an awareness of, other languages, cultures, ways of life, in and around our own environment. Without this creative tension every local culture and ethnicity in Europe degenerates and 'breeds reptiles of the mind'. I find the widespread parochial obsession with local history an unhealthy substitute.

I am not of course trying to locate some sort of European Utopia at some point in the past, before the division of Europe, its re-militarization and the Cold War. We have lost something which never existed in its pure form. Our heritage of creative diversity was always mixed up with intolerance, local racisms, wars and conflict. But we are entitled to see if we can reclaim positive aspects of our heritage, and try to salvage what hasn't disappeared altogether.

There has always been destruction side by side with creativity, but when early this century schoolchildren in Wales were beaten for speaking Welsh at school and Polish schoolchildren in Prussian Poland conducted a series of long and bitter school strikes to keep the subject of religious instruction in their own language in an otherwise German-taught curriculum,[10] a process of destruction of Europe's ethnographic and cultural ecology was accelerating. Abhorrence of untidy diversity and the regulation of uniformity had become principles of administration of whole states.

These principles became so much second nature to the administrators that in my native Holland in 1940 and 1941, when the country was already occupied, native civil servants created the most comprehensive and sophisticated population registration system anywhere in Europe, so that Eichmann could testify in Jerusalem that the deportations of Jews from that country were no trouble at all. *And those civil servants didn't know what they were doing* until it was too late. (This is what makes documents like the PTT WINTEX scenarios so shocking.)

Europe's myriad streams had become stagnant national pools of administration where reptiles bred; reptiles which became some big and a great many little Fascist monsters. What were those first few post-war years like in Europe, after the reptiles had, through mass murders, disruption and devastation, brought the destruction of Europe's always-precarious eco-system of multi-ethnic, multi-lingual, multi-faith, multi-everything life and culture to a conclusion of a sort? I am just too young, I didn't see it. I can only go by other people's reports.

In 1947 a Dutch author, Gerard Reve, published a novel *De Avonden* ('The Evenings'). While it was still in manuscript form, the country's literary establishment had already declared it to be an Official Masterpiece and awarded it a major prize. The country's real establishment – i.e. just about everybody else – raised its finger, went tut-tut, and declared it to be a scandal, a blasphemy, an obscenity, the greatest piece of trash ever published and beyond doubt a direct communication from the Antichrist. There was also a group of people nobody took much notice of because they hadn't been invented yet, the teenagers. They *read* the book, and stopped reading because they could not face what they were reading, or read it anyway.

But what did this terribly subversive publication actually say? Very little. The story (but it seems hardly a story) describes how a young office clerk, Frits Egters, kills time in his evenings after work in the winter of 1946 in Amsterdam. Two hundred pages of banal little non-events. Frits Egters moves in a cosy, safe little world, goes through all the motions, planning and calculating how to fill in the time when he isn't at work or asleep with whatever trivia come to hand. Not a single swearword, no sex, no reference to anything shocking. No past, no future. It is an unnerving book to read, even after forty years. It doesn't say things; it doesn't say anything, and it is a sustained scream of despair.

In 1947 someone in Holland had seen that the moment at

which the process of recovery, the healing of Europe, should have began had already been lost. There was enough to eat again, there was fuel in the winter. Nobody slept in the streets despite a desperate housing shortage in Holland; and there was no past and no future. The reptiles were back again and they didn't hear Frits Egters's screaming, for reptiles have no ears.

One year later the Englishman George Orwell had sussed out what exactly the reptiles were up to, what they were constructing. Europe was to be shared between just two stagnant pools: Oceania and Eurasia. But I am not going to quote Orwell. In 1982 the Hungarian Geörgy Dalos wrote a politically sophisticated, pessimistic and very funny sequel to *1984*, called *1985* (published in English by Pluto Press). O'Brian (Winston Smith's torturer) noted in *1985* that the population was totally lunatic after decades of war propaganda, which is not surprising with communiqués like this one:

The Oceanian News Agency ONA is authorized by the competent authority to state the following: certain Eurasian press organs are spreading lying and tendentious rumours in connection with the alleged 'destruction' of the Oceanian Air Force over the Canary Islands. In this connection the Oceanian News Agency ONA is obliged to state: these lying Eurasian rumours are a pure invention and lack any basis. This in no way contributes to good relations between the two combatant countries . . .

We may well curse the superpowers, but is that all there is to it? We are in Europe, where things are supposed to be complicated and ambiguous. Here is a parable out of Günther Grass's novel *Hundejahre* ('Dog Years') from 1963.

In Nickelswalde, near Danzig, east of the Vistula estuary, there has for many centuries been a cornmill where the Matern dynasty ground flour for the neighbourhood. Miller Anton Matern, through a lifetime of carrying bags of corn and flour on his right shoulder, has a flattened and strangely developed right ear. It is deaf to everything, except to what goes on inside the bags. Anton Matern can listen to the corn weevils inside the bags: he hears them move about; by listening he knows how many there are in each bag, which species, and even how many dead and how many living ones. And what is more, he can hear the weevils talking amongst each other. Miller Matern thus has access to privileged information, which is highly useful to the local farming community.

Via miller Matern the weevils foretell the best times to sow and what to sow, they predict the weather and fluctuations in the exchange rates of the currency, the Danzig gulden.

Early in 1945 miller Matern and his wife and his sister abandon the mill in Nickelswalde to flee from the advancing Russian armies. Miller Matern carries with him a 20 lb bag of flour. The ship with refugees is sunk by a mine in the Baltic Sea, and Matern is the only survivor, still holding on to the bag of flour, and he manages to reach the Western sector. Danzig becomes Gdansk, and the miller from Nickelswalde finds an abandoned cornmill near Krefeld where he sets up shop. But he doesn't grind corn any more. He listens to the weevils' prophecies and becomes a kind of consultant, first for the local neighbourhood, and as his fame spreads people from all over the country come to see him. The East German weevils advise the West German bankers, industrialists, union leaders and press barons. Axel Springer is told: 'three million illiterates will read the *Bildzeitung*[11] over breakfast every day'.

The East German weevils, which survived the gruelling journey where thousands died, built the newly established Federal Republic's 'Wirtschafswunder', the amnesiac state with its post-war economic 'miracle'. The weevils are quite impartial, they prophesy for anyone, but the planners of the newly created GDR find out too late, and when they finally make the pilgrimage to the mill near Krefeld they find it cordoned off by West German officials to prevent access by those from the East. Hence business can prosper on the West's unequal terms.[12]

The German for corn weevils is 'Mehlwurmen'. Grass tells a story about worms. The post-war economic miracle is like a bad apple full of worms, and the badness is home-grown and interacts with the system of division of Europe. I'll embroider a little on the theme.

Because the weevils from the East have been cordoned off in the mill near Krefeld in the West, West Berlin, which is in the East, must be cordoned off too, and the wall is built on 13 August 1961. A British officer noted at the time: 'When twenty-four hours had passed peacefully we relaxed and thanked God that the danger of war, triggered by the threat of an East German collapse, had passed.'[13] And Paul Oestreicher observed that the growing East German economic and political stability provided by the wall was one factor that had made Willi Brandt's *Ostpolitik* possible.[14] Oestreicher wrote this without implied bitterness, and it is quite possible to look at the event in this way. But recently I heard a Czech say, with a great deal of bitterness, that the 'normalization' (the Russian invasion in 1968) paved the way for detente, for detente requires consolidation within each bloc. And I remember that in 1981 the Western banking community was getting decidedly uneasy about the rise of Solidarnosc. The bankers made the pilgrimage to the weevils from the Vistula estuary and started to drop hints to the effect that their loans to Poland would be better secured if Solidarnosc were somehow brought under control.

From the point of view of Europe and the Europeans the Cold War is not *about* anything at all. It is a petrified piece of posturing between two superpower systems. It is a total falsification of whatever real problems we have, or had in the past. Its *effect* was initially one of indefinite postponement of the healing of our wounds and losses in 1945. Its subsequent effects were to set up a false frame of reference which made it impossible to come properly to terms with our own ambiguous and traumatic pasts and to make truly constructive contributions to the needs of the Third World.

The Cold War and superpower system in Europe has a peculiar and utterly reactionary 'deep structure', one which has been grafted on a strictly European growth. It is a mystification, a deeply ideological nineteenth-century form of rewriting European history. It has an element of vulgar social Darwinism, where the essence of the European experience came to be perceived as an endless and relentless struggle between the collective peoples of the East and the West. Each side came to perceive the other as an inevitable threat. The bipolar Cold War system has been grafted on to that older view of 'Teutons' and 'Slavs', more and more seen as races rather than cultural categories, who struggled for the same patch of space to live.[15]

Serious historians of Europe have been demonstrating patiently that this 'Teutons *v.* Slavs' notion is in fact historically counterfeit.[16] But this intellectual reptile is still at large in popular accounts. You find it as an unstated assumption all over the place, even where people observe 'the East' with a great deal of genuine interest and sympathy.

Timothy Garton Ash, for example, in an otherwise very good article about the new problems, issues and complexities in East Europe generated by the Chernobyl disaster, wrote:

. . . It is even more difficult to determine how 'the West' can best encourage or influence internal developments [in East Europe] which are so gradual, unplanned, subterranean and diverse . . .[17]

In spite of the careful phrasing, his underlying axiom is that it is 'the West's' business to 'encourage or influence' things, that 'the West' has a kind of *mission* in 'the East'.

And now I can finally put my finger on what is wrong with Mertes's notion of 'hate-free zones in Europe' in *NATO Review*. It is the right idea, but in quite the wrong place, and therefore the wrong idea. Mertes assumes that the 'hatred between peoples, nations and systems' is an East–West issue. *It is not*. Mertes is assuming *causes* for hatred between the peoples of East and West, and he is therefore either regurgitating Cold War propaganda or he is illiterate in European history and is falling back on the discredited 'Teutons *v.* Slavs' deeply ideological falsification of the European experience – a racist theory which legitimated the Nazi project. Asking for hate-free zones between *system* is verbal garbage: systems can be made compatible or not, as the case

may be, since systems are *things*. And if you say, in the East–
West context, that you would like to see 'hate-free zones',
between *states* or alliances of states, you are in effect engaged
in the Dalos–Orwellian project of 'contributing to good relations between the combatant states'. Mertes unwittingly
issued an ONA press release.

The supposed entities, 'East' and 'West', are ideological
fictions, products of the reptile house. Certainly, the military
alliances of the blocs have to be dealt with, along with nuclear
weapons, in the emergency agenda of our time. Even so, we
must take care, for if our campaigning activities against the
blocs are given the wrong type of emphasis it is possible to
reinforce these categories.

The Cold War categories of 'East' and 'West' are useless
for any constructive purposes. One stated aim of the European peace movements, in 1980, was to ignore these categories and to begin to act as if they did not exist: 'We must
learn to be loyal, not to "East" or "West", but to each
other.'[18] Authentic differences (which are sometimes evi-
denced by real loves and hates) do not coincide with the
East/West line on the map. They are rather situated in large
neighbourhoods which overlap and flow into each other. And
'Europe' itself is changing and is uncertain of its identity.

In my local library in the London Borough of Croydon
there are shelves full of books in languages such as German,
French and Polish, and also Bengali, Urdu, Hindi and
Vietnamese. West Berlin has a Turkish community of some
400,000 people. In Brussels Arabic-speaking parents send
their children to French-speaking schools, and the French-
speaking parents tend to dislike that and send their children
to Flemish-speaking schools instead. Two years ago the first
pan-Frisian Congress to re-establish Frisian cultural identity
and language was held in Leeuwarden in the northern
Netherlands, with participants from Frisia in Holland itself
but also from northern Germany and Denmark, mainly
farmers. And on Sunday afternoons Dutch radio broadcasts
programmes in Serbo-Croat, Greek, Portuguese, Arabic,
Spanish, Turkish, Italian – the list is not complete.

I am picking examples at random. I have no overview of what is happening in West Europe. In the real neighbourhoods of the cities we cannot always pride ourselves on our 'hate-free zones'. Yet against stacks of evidence – poverty, ugly racisms, genuine cultural conflicts – I feel it in my bones that in my corner of Europe, through an apparently contradictory process which might be called 'de-Europeanization', a new but authentic European way of life is being created again in places like Bradford and Brixton.

West Europe has perhaps become ethnically and linguistically more complex than any part of Central or East Europe. Once the East/West division has been overcome, how will the peoples relate to each other, not as ideologists, but as actual neighbours? Which 'Europe' and for which 'Europeans'? And if Zdena Tomin is right in suspecting that 'the Iron Curtain is but a pile of decaying ideological rubbish' (see p. 177), as any borough environmental health officer will tell you, decaying rubbish (ideological) should be dealt with and can't be assumed to go away by itself. It might breed serious public health hazards: reptiles, weevils and what not. One option is to incinerate the lot, decontaminate the ground, and start from scratch again. But is such a thing possible in ambiguous Europe? Can we ever make an entirely fresh start? What is the peace movement doing amidst these rubbish piles?

We have not only been protesting and demonstrating, we have also made immense efforts to build a 'peace infrastructure'. This infrastructure consists of the various ways peace groups and organizations and related social forces in different countries meet, exchange information and ideas, or organize combined activities. It is a fragile *ad hoc* structure of a few committees, informal direct links between countries and individuals with an internationalist outlook, who help where they can through passing on messages and information, visits to other countries and translation work.

It is through this, largely informal, network that the information about the peace camp held in Srednji Vrh in 1984

reached me. I have no idea how many hands these few dup-
licated sheets passed through before a friend in Britain mailed
them to me. Our resources are so meagre that we can't afford
to hook up to the 'information processing society'. Our
communications technology is partly of the early twentieth
century (telephone and postal service – not always reliable
though, because of interference by the zealous security
services of both sides), and partly of the eighteenth century,
when messages go from hand to hand. And sometimes it is
like the days of Marco Polo when the only way to find out
the truth about what people a few hundred miles away are
thinking and doing is to go there and find out on the spot;
perhaps by hitchhiking across Europe. That is Europe's
peace infrastructure in the technical sense.

In my own experience, in a British group which specializes
in maintaining contact with people in Hungary, I am again
and again astonished to find how peaceniks so far apart and
with such limited means of communication tend to have so
much the same outlook on things. This hints all the time at a
wider concept of 'peace infrastructure', a much more pervasive and yet rather intangible one.

The fifty or so participants at Srednji Vrh set up a regional
committee of groups from Carinthia in Austria, Friuli in
Italy and Slovenia in Yugoslavia. They had an outing to a
place where they felt particularly at home, the small area of
no-man's-land between the three countries, and held a picnic
there. And they issued a letter to the governments. It dealt
with the need for nuclear-free and demilitarized zones in
Europe, and then:

Part of the meeting dealt with the situation of national minorities.
All participants agreed that peace can only be achieved in countries
and regions where different ethnic groups are living together in a
climate of equality, mutual respect and recognition of minority
rights. Therefore the participants appeal to you to do everything to
create such a climate. We especially request you not to tolerate
measures which would mean worsening the situation of national
minorities concerning schools, cultural and economic fields and
would be put through against the declared will of these people.

A note on the use of language. In East and Central Europe people tend to say 'national' where we would say 'ethnic', 'linguistic' or 'cultural'. In that part of the world there has never been a neat correlation between states and nations.

I believe that I am in tune with the spirit of this statement when I do not interpret it as one which only applies to that particular corner of south-central Europe. I would only argue that this demand ought to be addressed to a wider constituency than governments. These people who met in Slovenia are telling us: we, a bunch of people who campaign against nuclear weapons and who are trying to overcome the division of Europe, have arrived at the conclusion that it matters a great deal for Europe what happens and what the long-term future is going to be like in places like Britain's multi-ethnic inner cities.

I find the core of everything I have been thinking about once again in a novel. It is by one of those English writers at the edge of things who put down in a novel of absolutely stunning perception what is, and has been, going on in Europe.

In Rex Warner's *The Aerodrome* (first published in 1941), an English, very English, village is so deeply parochial that it has fallen into a kind of incestuous degeneracy. Everything is sordid, squalid and decrepit in the villagers' lives and doings. Outside, on the edge of the village, is the new aerodrome. This is a world of discipline and technology, the Air Force is in control of things. They know what they are about, they are in control of themselves, their environment, their emotions and relationships, they have a sense of purpose. A *clean* world. Cleanliness makes free – *Reinheit macht frei*. The hero-narrator of the story flips back and forth between the two worlds in his loyalty and attachment, like those ribbed plastic pictures again, one object with two images.

The aerodrome, being the stronger entity, exerts gradually more and more control over the village and begins to order and cleanse the sluttish community by policing and intervening in its affairs. But somehow it doesn't work out that way, for the village's messy affairs begin to intertwine more and more with those of the airmen. The story is resolved when it is revealed that various leading characters of the aerodrome, including even the Air Vice-Marshal, the aerodrome's mastermind, are members of the village families through sordid relationships linked by crime. The death of the Air Vice-Marshal is the last of a series of murders, the aerodrome disintegrates, and the village 'wins'.

In an introduction to a 1982 edition a vague kind of conclusion is drawn by Anthony Burgess:

... we are in a location that is universal, not just English. And yet tha language breathes England – not just the flowers and the grass but also the common-sense pragmatism and decency which will defeat, we think, any encroachment of totalitarian aerodromes.

This makes *The Aerodrome* seem like a humane and forgiving book. But such an assessment misses the point because it overlooks a curious imbalance in the book. The village and its people appear in their full living three-dimensionality. The aerodrome and its people are less developed and gain reality through increasing interaction with the village. And outside that, the wider world is virtually non-existent. There are a few references to its existence, but they make no difference to the substance of the story. They could just as well have been left out. To all intents and purposes *there is no outside world*.

The aerodrome had grown out of the village and grew back into it again. To begin with, the aerodrome seemed to represent a shiny, clean and above all *new* world of the future, but it was a fake. It was part of the village all the time. That is the key to the story.

The Aerodrome is a mercilessly clinical analysis (even though it is funny in places) of the process of reptile-breeding. It describes accurately how any ethnic group or culture in Europe which ceases to exchange with other cultures at all levels will degenerate into an incestuous seediness and begin to produce monsters. Nationalism is one of the early symptoms. Tendencies to become genocidal, exterminist, are the most advanced stage. Star Wars (SDI) is the United States's aerodrome, to give a particularly illuminating but not quite European example.

It is easy to be deceived by the book's poetic ending. But there is no indication anywhere to lead you to believe that the final revelations of past lies and deceit founded on crime – an incestuous marriage which is also a bond between the village and the aerodrome turns out to be not incestuous after all – cannot themselves be lies and deceit. The village didn't have any 'common-sense pragmatism and decency'. It had closed in on itself and made itself mad. The aerodrome was not defeated but got absorbed deeper into the village's fabric.

The Aerodrome is the best piece of merciless analysis of the dark side of the European experience I know of, and it lies at the heart of all those things I have been trying to understand so far. This is what we must set the infrastructure of peace against.

Setting out to try to make some sense of 'Europe' is to bite off more than anyone can chew. It is all about things which cannot, and which I believe *ought not*, to be worked out by an individual. I offer a few tentative conclusions.

At the heart of Europe's screwed-upness lies the 'aerodrome process'. The superpowers are villages with aerodromes (and each one has a major European heritage, of good and bad things), and locally, at the level of states and nations, and even more locally – especially in the West, in the multi-ethnic cities – the same process is always in danger of being reproduced (is actually being reproduced in places) which feeds back into the Cold War system in all sorts of complex ways.

To overcome this is a project of an entirely different order from demonstrating against missiles. It is the essentially cultural task of opening up Europe's diversity to exchange and interaction.

The political entities 'East' and 'West' must be overcome to make Europe's demilitarization a lasting reality. But these political categories are negative ones; they are on the emergency agenda of the things we are campaigning *against*. They are such artificial entities that you can't do much with them in terms of repairing Europe. After all, Denmark and Sicily are both in the political 'West'. Does that mean anything at all outside the NATO context? It is hard to believe that a Bulgarian Muslim and a citizen of East Berlin have much in common, even though both live in the political 'East'. Or in terms of geography: 'Communist' Prague lies well to the west of technically 'neutral', but in practice 'Free West' Vienna.

Or a fascinating political game: if Norman Tebbit happened to be Polish instead of English, where would you have found him at the negotiating table in the Lenin shipyard in Gdansk – next to Walesa or opposite? What would the UK government have done in the face of a British Solidarnosc labour movement? And if you are black and unemployed in Brixton, does 'East–West' mean anything at all?

All other things being equal, a Europe without the superpowers could lead to a variety of outcomes. A hundred flowers *might* bloom, but the treacherous 'Europe for the Europeans' option is open too. Europe could become another superpower, a neo-colonialist bloc. Or the economically stronger capitalist West could be a force of social and cultural destruction in the East European countries, and at the end of the day people there would have exchanged one bum deal for another. It can even be argued that the superpower in each half has, over the years, fulfilled a peacekeeping function *inside* each sphere of influence.

The peace movements' international communications structure is making heroic efforts to encourage a new Europe of true neighbourhood, but our fragile links cannot cope with the type, and especially the volume, of traffic involved in questions such as these. We must rely on a much wider context of exchanges. I am particularly thinking of what I call 'Europe's storytellers', of past and present: poets, novelists, playwrights, film-makers, and their essential companions, the translators. The people who make and transmit products of the imagination. These are the people who can repair our history and shape visions for the future to sustain and give content to the bleak day-to-day campaigning reality. We in the peace movements must not think that we can do it all ourselves, or we end up like some of the more conceited Dutchmen who rewrite the Book of Genesis: When God put his tools away on the evening of the seventh day, he had quite forgotten to make Holland. On the morning of the eighth day the Dutch got their shovels out and started digging in the clay to do the job themselves. And they have been at it ever since. *But where did they get the shovels from?*

Notes

1. Stella Gibbons; *Cold Comfort Farm*, first published 1932.
2. Derived from e.g. CREL (Central Region Events List) of HQ AFCENT nr. SHOPE 1712.13/ACPXCX/S 682/80 d.d. 290280 or Air-raid Planning List of AAFCE (Allied Air Forces Central Europe).
3. The documents were obtained by the anti-militarist action group Onkruit in a raid on a civil-defence bunker and a military communications bunker on the Dutch coast. Some have been reproduced in the 'samizdat'-type book *Bunker in – Bunkerbuit*, Amsterdam, 1984; some circulate informally in photocopy form. The documents have been publicly exhibited in a travelling exhibition, and were later auctioned off (several dustbin-liner sacks full) at a large party open to all.

    The authenticity of the documents was inadvertently admitted by Major Struycker of the Dutch Defence Ministry, but half an hour later withdrawn again – possibly after furious telephone calls from NATO headquarters in Brussels (*Vrij Nederland*, 1 October 1983).
4. Robert Edwin Herzstein, *When Nazi Dreams Come True*, London, Sphere, 1982.
5. SCV/W/80/42 – VERTROUWELIJK. Voorlopige Basisgegevens schadebeeld(en) PTT-Districtenspel Wintex/Cimex '81 ('Civil Defence Staff – Confidential. Provisional basic information on overall damage in the PTT District Simulation Wintex/Cimex '81').
6. Alois Mertes, 'East–West revelations: the political dimension', *Nato Review*, No. 1, February 1985.
7. This information is becoming dated. Romania is now politically

and economically in such a state that a wholesale exodus of the German communities is taking place, bringing to a close in places a history of settlement going back to the thirteenth century (*Labour Focus on Eastern Europe*, Vol. 8, No. 2, May 1986).

8. *Wurzelwerk*, January 1985.

9. Benedict Anderson, *Imagined Communities: The Origin and Spread of Nationalism*, London, Verso, 1983.

10. John J. Kulczycki, *School Strikes in Prussian Poland 1901–1907: the Struggle over Bilingual Education*, New York, 1981.

11. The *Bildzeitung* is very much the same type of tabloid paper as the *Sun* in Britain. The name means: 'Picture Paper'.

12. Under a kind of 'thirty-five-year rule' a 1953 memorandum by the West German career diplomat Richard Meyer von Aschenbach has been made public. This memorandum argued a level-headed and persuasive case for taking up Stalin's offer of a united neutral Germany with free elections. Adenauer was terrified by this memorandum, and ensured that it was immediately spirited away and remained secret, for, as has been discovered in British Foreign Office papers, he noted that if this memorandum became public it would have 'catastrophic consequences for his political position' (*Der Spiegel*, 11 August 1986).

13. Quoted in the *Guardian*, 11 August 1986.

14. Paul Oestreicher, ibid.

15. This distortion in European history writing is described in detail in, e.g., Hermann Schreiber, *Teuton and Slav*, London, Constable, 1965. Even central European archaeology was politicized.

16. See e.g. the collection by historians from East and West: K. Bosl and others, *Eastern and Western Europe in the Middle Ages*. London, Thames & Hudson, 1970.

17. *Spectator*, 5 July 1986.

18. END Appeal, of 28 April 1980, in *Protest and Survive*, ed. E. P. Thompson and Dan Smith, Penguin Books, 1980.

7 Zdena Tomin: Which Side? The Dreams of an Exile

Much has been written about the significance of dreams, even though, in the everyday succession of dreary mornings, most people don't bother to ponder them. For an exile, however, dreams are an almost constitutive part of his or her experience, and there are quite a few that are generally shared among fellow exiles – by 'exile' I mean a person who has been forced to leave or prevented from returning to his or her country of origin for political reasons.

At an early stage of my own exile-hood (in 1980), my dreams were almost identical to those a Chilean friend used to have, but she assured me that the worst ones would ease off with time. She was right: I no longer suffer those unbearable guilt-ridden nightmares of the first months. I don't even want to describe them any longer; suffice it to say that they had to do with all the despairs of a traitor, a deserter who had left his friends behind in combat.

Now and then I still get a dream that is painful and makes me toss about the bed in sobs of an almost Russian intensity. It is a well-known exile dream: there is a fence, wall, barrier, frontier; behind the frontier, there is Home; one's heart leaps over the barrier, one's body cannot. The thing with me is that Home is no longer defined in terms of one country, sometimes it's Czechoslovakia, sometimes it's England; on whatever side of that fence the dream puts me, I pine for the other, mortified by the thought that I can never see it again.

But most of my dreams have become strangely lovely, and thoroughly mixed, as grain harvested from different fields gets mixed in a mill. When I sleep, I can walk across Trafalgar Square with Michael Heseltine who makes sense speaking in an impeccable if grumpy Czech, make a sharp turn left and walk up a winding medieval street to the Prague Castle, take a sledge-ride down the hill with a bunch of old schoolmates dressed in Wimpy uniforms, cross the river and find myself, with only mild surprise, in Rome chased by an odd KGB agent who turns out to be my old music teacher, and end up among the dunes on Harlech beach with my mother calling me home for dinner in a true Hackney English and looking hurt if I remind her that she never, in life, spoke anything but an ordinary middle-Bohemian Czech. All this in one dream, painted in warm colours and deep lights, such as, in real life, can be found only before or after a summer thunderstorm. It is a wonderful world and I hate waking up.

In my waking hours I am a bit of a freak, like those people who can whistle and sing simultaneously. My thoughts often conduct themselves in English and in Czech at the same time; it may well be an advanced mental process, but it wears me out, especially as it is not only a linguistic problem but also a competition between two different ways of thinking.

Yet, on the whole, I suppose I am lucky. It is generally thought that a politically involved person, forced into exile, irretrievably loses the very backbone of her involvement in life and sooner or later becomes a walking anachronism, sadly out of touch with the Cause yet clinging to it, unable to let go and find another. I was terrified that it would happen to me. To some degree it did, certainly on the outside: it is now some seven years since I was, in Prague, one of the three spokespersons for the Charter 77 human-rights movement, yet whenever I give a talk I am introduced to the audience as the 'spokesperson of Charter 77'. Having explained that I am one no longer and that I have actually come from London, I can feel that it is a bit of a let-down for the audience, and wish I had some status to my name. (I then have to be unashamedly personal in my talk, and am always humbled by the readiness of English people to share one's intimate experience and one's personal political passions.)

That I am not suffering from any Loss of Cause lies, I think, entirely with the cause itself, the ambition for freedom, for justice, for democracy. My realization that my cause was not peculiar to Czechoslovakia was not a sudden revelation. Rather, in a process of slow amazement, I was reassured to find out that I (like millions of Czechs, Poles or Hungarians) do not have and never have had any other cause than the general ideals shared by quite a few million born-and-bred British, French, Swedish, etc., citizens – even though, personally, I grew up on Stalin's left shoe.

The monstrously huge monument of the Generalissimo stood on the Letna hill overlooking the river and its bridges, the spires of the Old Town and, on winter days when the trees have shed their leaves, the silhouette of Prague Castle. Between the ages of fourteen and seventeen, I often played truant from school, comfortably seated on the well-moulded, sun-warmed granite of Stalin's left shoe, reading (and scribbling) poetry.

All that time the monument was due for demolition, as the days of Stalinism were over. But it was more difficult to dismantle than it was to build, demolition projects failing to ensure that the entire hill's structure would not collapse into the river. I did not have to hurry my reading, and I was never disturbed; nobody came to pay a tribute. In the magnificent rooms inside and under the monument only potatoes were stored and left to decay in their wet sacks. It was a magical place, perfect for a gradual recovery from the shock the disclosure of the Stalinist terror gave me (born below the poverty line and with a Communist father, I was an ardent Red Pioneer until then). There I would dream about the world beyond the horizon, reading Apollinaire or Whitman or Lermontov or sonnets by one William Shakespeare; anything I could lay my hands on.

By the time that Stalin's shoe was finally sledgehammered, or whatever was done to it, the era of the sixties was budding, and soon I had no problems or doubts whatsoever. I did not join the Party – that I rejected for ever – but I could see no reason why socialism couldn't be shaped into a democratic society, if we all felt strongly about it, if we all fought the conservative Communist and, above all, the censor. (My heart aches when I remember 1964, 5, 6, 7, 8 . . . I can't say it better than Milan Kundera: 'This happy marriage of culture and life, of creative achievement and the people, has marked the revolts of Central Europe with a beauty so inimitable that it will always cast a spell over those who lived through those times.') Only I would not call the Prague Spring a mere revolt; I still think that we were pretty damn near to creating a society with a human face, outside Communism and capitalism. But I had better stop right here, or I would launch into a long tirade of 'if onlies' and 'why on earths?'

My first journey to the 'West' was with a small group of students and scholars. Then, as early as 1964 and for the first time since the war, we were starting an exchange with the University of Heidelberg in West Germany. I couldn't have been more excited, I felt as though I was on a mission, even if my German was still very poor.

A cab-driver in Heidelberg asked me, inevitably, where I was from, and when I duly answered I was from Prague, Czechoslovakia, he almost killed us both, trying to embrace me while driving. 'Oh I am so glad for you, Fräulein,' he exclaimed, 'you are saved!' Watching my uncomprehending face, he asked – 'You are not going back there, are you?!' I laughed but couldn't make him see what was funny, and he parted from me very grudgingly. But he would have had his revenge if he could have seen me only a couple of hours later making a public spectacle of myself.

I was twenty-three at that time, and I had never eaten a single whole banana. A few could then be bought on the market in Prague, but I had a one-year-old son and what I could buy, he got; I just bit off the heads and tails. So, in Heidelberg, I bought a whole bunch, a dozen or so beautiful, ripe bananas, carried them to the nearest bench on the University Square and, seeing nothing, hearing nothing, ate all of them but one. Waking up from the trance, I found myself surrounded by a crowd of West Germans who watched with fascination this obviously well-fed, well-dressed young woman, stuffing herself with a nauseating quantity of bananas. I could have died of shame; yet even the last fruit, eaten in the comparative privacy of a youth hostel, tasted of sweet luxury.

For quite some time I thought that the 'West' had little to offer apart from an occasional banana or a pair of jeans, an occasional good book, film, play or art exhibition, and an occasional free and futile discussion on politics or philosophy. (Lord, how I wish I could have back all those hours spent in arguments about variations of Marxism! I'd use them to plant trees or to visit my old aunts in the village before they all die out, ever so quietly, taking a wealth of knowledge with them.)

I wasn't really looking, for I was very arrogant. I reckoned that everybody in the 'West' had just about what they wanted and were playing revolutions out of sheer boredom, while we in Prague were the unobtrusive builders of a new democratic world. I mistook both the Soviet Union and the United States for mildly stupid giants losing their last imperialist teeth and becoming basically benign . . . That era of confidence and blissful ignorance couldn't have lasted more than three or four years of my life, but in retrospect it seems like ages.

Since the Soviet invasion of Czechoslovakia in 1968 (which paved the way to Soviet–American detente!) I've been through some punitive if efficient 'schooling', both as an anonymous inhabitant of an occupied and crippled country and as a 'dissident' with a name and address best known to the police. But I wonder whether I could have completed my 'political education', or closed a full circle of my particular life, if – more by a random work of fate than by some elaborate KGB plan – I hadn't been 'chosen' for exile instead of imprisonment.

If I had not come to live in Britain, if I had not seen (with disbelieving eyes at first) the class system at work, if I had not had to try to accommodate myself to it, I doubt if I could have resurrected the wounded socialist buried alive deep in my mind. And I could have cherished freedom only as a Utopian dream, as an abstract or purely personal value, for the rest of my life, had I not seen it (with all its limitations) at work in Britain, France, the United States; had I not lived it.

It is uncanny what similar mistakes we make on both sides of the Divide, what similar rhetorics we use, always ready to reject Socialism for Freedom, or Freedom for Socialism. (I can get an easy round of applause if I mock the – in many aspects perfectly mockable – British Freedom; and I confess with shame that I have not always resisted the temptation, while my best friends were sitting in police dungeons in Prague or Brno for breathing a word of plain truth.) Fortunately, we don't really mean it. The numbers of people actually pining for the restoration of capitalism in Central and Eastern Europe, and the numbers of people willing to do without fundamental liberties, democratic institutions, the ballot and election rights in Western Europe, are minimal; such people form negligible minorities. While the state ideologies of East and West have become skin-deep and purely instrumental, the real sets of social and political values vital to most people are clearly converging.

My old suspicion that the Iron Curtain is but a pile of decaying ideological rubbish, which has to be held upright by the extensive military hardware of the two 'blocs' and by the mutual blackmail of the nuclear threat, has grown considerably since I came to live in Britain. On good days, this gives sustenance to my strangely incurable optimism; on bad days, to angry despair. Maybe we are too far gone, maybe we fear the bomb too much to think about sensible alternatives. (That various combinations of socialism, democracy and 'traditional' freedom are not a case of having your cake and eating it, is evident in Scandinavia, perhaps precisely because they managed, by a mixture of geographical luck, a strong concept of social justice and good political sense, to remain largely outside the US–USSR divide.)

My optimism is nourished by the growing awareness, among Europe's democratic opposition to warmongering and injustice, of the connections between the division of Europe, the arms race and the campaigns for nuclear disarmament. (Also between Charter 77, END and CND; Solidarnosc and the miners' strike; peace and police status – of such 'small connections' there are many more.) Detente from below is not to be sneezed at: it may just bring Europe to its senses, if we do not abandon it for lesser strategies.

All right, I am a dreamer. I dream a lot about Britain too, since I have come to love it (especially as England, Wales and Scotland), since English is the language I write in. I do dream of a day when it would no longer be possible for a Conservative leader to rebuff the Labour Party by accusing it of wanting to establish 'the same shabby, look-alike, totalitarian states they have in Eastern Europe'. Not because the Labour Party does not deserve any criticism, but because the argument is blatantly incorrect and hypocritical.

East Europeans do not 'have' totalitarian states; that Central and Eastern Europe suffer under totalitarianism is primarily a result of post-war agreements between the strongest victors, and of the Cold War politics that followed. And though there is a terrible drabness in Romania, though much of Poland is shabby and poor, though freedom and gaiety are gone from Czechoslovakia and Hungarians could do enormously better, some of the most shabby, drab, uniform and poor districts can still be found in England; street after street of the same dilapidated houses, dusty shops, bad food, insufficient health care, hopelessness and misery.

In other words, my dream is about pooling our resources and ideas, instead of bashing each other on the head with sticks that aren't even ours (though manufacturing our own sticks is clearly not the answer). Maybe I dream so much because I am an exile, because I have by now lived under different sets of ideologies, met two sets of people with the same needs and wishes, and two versions of militant conservative establishments producing opposite enemy-images yet actually supporting each other very well.

I can dream out the blackest of comedies: months after a global or 'limited' nuclear war, when it is safe to move about again, dozens of high-ranking government members and their scouts will climb out of their bunkers, travel to the least damaged landscape (somewhere in Switzerland, I shouldn't wonder) and shake hands over a glass of vintage, pre-nuclear champagne – and over millions of our rotting bodies. And it isn't my favourite nightmare. The only good thing about it is that it stops me being ashamed of dreaming aloud and even suggesting that my dreams are made of some real stuff. That the human, social, historical, and in a true sense political conditions for the crumble and fall of the Iron Curtain are here: that it is a workable dream.

8   Jiri Dienstbier: Pax Europeana: A View from the East

Clearly it is true that it is not possible to change history. The cruel Jewish joke sums it up: 'When will there be a complete rehabilitation? When it becomes possible to make Jews out of soap.'

Every war has seen murder, the devastation of cities, the burning of villages, the raping of women, the violation of borders and the creation of many thousands of refugees. What happens does not occur in obedience to the rules of justice, but is determined by the advancing armies. The final victory establishes the 'final principles'. The last war was especially cruel both in its course and in its consequences.

This applies also to the question of state borders. States always have borders somewhere. Now they have their present ones. It would not make a lot of sense if we demanded back Lusatia and the whole of Silesia, which for many years were under the Czech crown. No Czechs live there any more.

Nor can anything be done to reverse the population transfers.* Not because it was German Nazism which started the war, for reasons for which the Germans themselves know that they were responsible. Their leaders attempted to Germanize or destroy the old national cultures and acted with great brutality. They lost, and reaped revenge, not justice. Women were expelled, too, and children who had not hurt anyone nor shouted out 'Heim ins Reich'.

* Jiri Dienstbier, writing from Prague, is reflecting upon the wholesale expulsion of the German minority from the Sudetenland and other parts of Czechoslovakia at the end of the Second World War. We reproduce here only the second part of his article. The first part includes significant reflections upon Central European history and the question of the two Germanys. The full text can be read in *Labour Focus on Eastern Europe*, Vol. 8, No. 1, Summer 1985.

These things were decided by the victorious great powers. They were carried out, not only by people who had reasons for revenge, even if they took it out on the whole family, but also by the worst elements of our nation. These people used the opportunity for their own enrichment and as a solace for their inferiority complexes, before, during and after the war – and even today.

However, those three million Germans have been gone now for forty years and nothing can be changed any more. What was done by the grandfathers and the fathers could only be reversed by inflicting new and pointless injustices on the children and the grandchildren, who had nothing to do with any of it . . .

Peace settlements are not realizations of dreams of love or friendship. All there is is a new balance of forces, born from the consequences of the preceding struggle. Strength, however, is not defined only by the number of people under arms, the quantity of bows and arrows, of cannon or nuclear warheads. The remark that Stalin made about the Pope's divisions ('How many divisions has the Pope?') and its occasional use amongst us, serves chiefly to demonstrate a particular cast of thought. Sometimes military weakness can be a political strength, as, for example, when the advantages of maintaining the neutrality of a particular country outweigh the costs of occupation for a potential aggressor, as was the case with Switzerland and Sweden during the Second World War.

For this reason it does not seem to me particularly important to enter into a debate about the technical aspects of the means of war. Past arms races at least took place in the realm of the possible. Nowadays useless weapons are poured forth in useless quantities. In both halves of Europe the useless rockets with nuclear warheads which are being put in place are not the cause but the consequence of the threat of war.

From a technical point of view, of course, these weapons are usable. Press the button and away they go; Europe's problems are solved, probably for all eternity. However, it serves no purpose to speculate on collective extinction; we must rather speculate about where and how it might be possible to unravel the Gordian knot, since it cannot these days be simply slashed through with a sword. We have to work out how to get out of the cul-de-sac, and eventually find ways of opening up new paths. Given the thousand-year-long experience of our civilization, every new path has probably been trodden by somebody at some time. We will even find buried treasure. Before we get there, however, we will have to get rid of both the most ancient and the newest prejudices.

If we are to succeed we must act in such a way that everybody else renounces their prejudices as well. The way to get them to do this is by means of an open and direct appeal – to offer the pipe of peace.

Recently much has been heard of Yalta. The spirit of Yalta is like all spirits. It flies wherever it wants. The most deceitful way of interpreting Yalta is to see it as an affirmation of the division of Europe into the spheres of influence of the two superpowers. That was something which was only consolidated afterwards. There was no agreement on the Polish question at Yalta, even if the concessions which Roosevelt and Churchill made to Stalin could be understood in that way. A compromise agreement was reached over Poland: that free elections after the end of the war would decide the form of government.

Nothing at all was said about the fate of Czechoslovakia, which had already defined its relationship to the Soviet Union by means of a treaty of friendship and post-war collaboration. Further developments did not evolve according to some fatalism or through agreements between the superpowers. Stalin had no precise notion of what Soviet influence in Central and Eastern Europe would entail, and he could not know how the situation would develop. He was pragmatic. In some cases he was evidently prepared to retreat (Iran, Greece or the Turkish border), or to accept a compromise solution if he was convinced that there would be sufficient guarantees of Soviet security (Finland), or to reach a satisfactory understanding when aggressive measures would lead to a greater danger than losing (Yugoslavia).

This did not mean that he hesitated when, for example, Czechoslovakia dropped into his lap through the initiative of a strong Communist Party, the political impotence of the non-communist parties, and the customary indecisiveness of President Beneš (who was, in any case, ill). We don't like to hear this kind of thing. We would much prefer to have had nothing to do with it, to have had bad luck, and, in short, to have been once again the victim of treacherous foreign powers. Numerous historians can produce convincing demonstrations as to the Soviet intention to annex Czechoslovakia. It would be amazing if Soviet policy had omitted to investigate this option thoroughly. Only a fool does not look into a whole gamut of possibilities.

Nevertheless, once we know the outcome, there is nothing simpler nor more one-sided than to lay out the reasons which inevitably led to it, and to exclude everything which was not realized. There is no absolute reason – neither the fact that it is 'the heart of Europe', nor our uranium, nor any other reason – that I can find which meant that Czechoslovakia could not have had the status of Yugoslavia, Finland or Austria, or have become a Czechoslovakia which would be neutral but bound by treaty to deliver 90 per cent of its uranium to the Soviet Union. (Just as long as it was only a matter of uranium!)

Not even the intervention of August 1968 has convinced me. We were not aiming to leave the Warsaw Pact or Comecon. We were not asking for neutrality, and, in the political sphere, rather than wanting a multi-party system, we thought of a democratic mechanism by which individuals and groups would express themselves as political subjects through the medium of existing institutions. Despite the fact that we showed such respect for the realities of the European situation, we were crushed.

All the existing national and international institutions were constituted in the post-war period as a consequence of the post-war development. While in the immediate post-war period even a lesser Soviet gain would have amounted to a success, in 1968 fears prevailed in Moscow that there was a danger of a lessening of Soviet influence. Whether you believe those fears to have been illusory or not will depend on your understanding of what the European 'peace' really is. If you believe that this peace is sustained by the presence of Soviet and American troops, the establishment of two incompatible economic mechanisms, and the tying of the internal political development of the European states to bloc politics – which in Eastern Europe has disrupted the functioning of society, through forcing the political system into a Stalinist mould, a model which developed in quite different conditions and traditions – then I am afraid that you are trapped in the vicious circle of a status quo, to which it might sometimes be possible to make peripheral cosmetic adjustments. Such a view is at odds with every social theory, including Marxism, and also has the disadvantage of having nothing to do with life, since on several occasions (and everywhere in the zone of direct Soviet control – with the exception of Bulgaria – through the medium of mass popular uprisings) people have demonstrated that this concept of the European 'peace' is not something which is beyond question.

While in Eastern Europe any attempt to revive the dynamic development of society through the liberation of internal creative forces is frustrated, in the Western part of our divided continent anyone who tries to challenge the obstacles to the unification of Europe is immediately assailed with accusations of wanting 'Finlandization'.

Firstly, the Finnish 'Finlandization' is an outstanding success of the policy of Paasikivi and his friends, who have succeeded in maintaining the independence and the right to free internal development of the small nation, which had not only just been defeated in a war with a huge neighbouring power, but had also in the past been a territorial part of that power for a long historical period. The quality of this success can only be fully appreciated if we bear in mind the tenacity with which Russia has always clung on to any territory which it has gained, and how much it dislikes letting go of any of it.

Secondly, small and large nations alike can only contribute to peace if they are prepared to respect the justified interests and fears of others, and particularly of their neighbours. It is essential for peace that the relations between neighbouring states are friendly ... Friendship with the Soviet Union is not some kind of concession or semi-vassalage for Finland, but a basic necessity. Friendly relations between the Soviet Union and Czechoslovakia are also a necessity, whatever condition they may be in at the moment. The situation is the same with regard to Britain and Germany. All this is generally understood throughout Central and Eastern Europe. If the populations of these countries were offered the status of Finland in a free referendum, they would vote for it with overwhelming enthusiasm, and would certainly prefer it to transferring their allegiance into the other camp.

Every status is defined by concrete conditions which do not apply anywhere else. The 'Finlandization' which is so much feared could not mean that Holland or West Germany, for example, would suddenly change into some kind of Finland on the other side of the continent. What its opponents would pejoratively describe as 'Finlandization' could only mean the unification of Europe, not as a beggar dependent on the whims of the two superpowers but as an association of free and equal nations, which would act on the world stage as a zone of peace. The Japanese example, with its economic and technical development unhindered by huge military exactions, shows that this is not just pie in the sky.

This sort of Europe would maintain military forces, but not in order to conquer anyone else or to strike terror into the hearts of the superpowers; none the less it would dispose of sufficient human and material potential to defend itself. It would be an inevitable condition for this state of affairs that it should be guaranteed by a treaty involving all the parties to this new arrangement of the Euro-American region, sustained by the strategic nuclear potential of the superpowers for a considerable period of time. At the moment this nuclear potential sustains the division of Europe, while the division in its turn justifies the continuance of the arms race. If the opposite conception were to be accepted in all or at least a majority of the European states, it would reverse the impulse towards militarization and initiate a process of the gradual restriction and reduction of the nuclear arsenals.

It is self-evident that this kind of development cannot take place on the basis of either an anti-Soviet or an anti-American orientation. Both powers must be offered guarantees that the drawing together and cooperation of the European powers require close and improving relations with both superpowers, particularly in the economic sphere, but also in cultural, social, scientific and other areas, and must involve free travel and contact between people.

Those who consider that Western military might is the only guarantee of peace are either (a) supporters of the untenable status quo in which we are presently condemned to live; (b) chronic pessimists who believe that there is an inevitable trend towards the totalitarianism of all humanity, consoling themselves with the thought that they will not live to see it; or (c) they must believe that at some stage, somehow or other, the military forces will be used and the Communist evil crushed. Such people are naïve.

It would, of course, be just as naïve to imagine that the process I have outlined will be straightforward. But, on the other hand, haven't we been caught up in its current for a long while already?

It is, however, necessary to take into account the objection, brought about by lack of confidence, uncertainty and loss of faith, that the new situation may not be any better than the old one. Under existing circumstances, one-sided disarmament, withdrawal from the blocs and unilateral declarations of neutrality are unrealistic. Peace will be a complex phenomenon or it will not come about at all, and the same is true of the paths that lead towards it.

It would certainly be ideal if all the governments from London to Warsaw accepted this kind of programme, and put it forward in a united way to the two superpowers. But this is not possible. There is, however, a vast open space to be filled by citizens' initiatives, the peace movement, political parties, churches, professional bodies. There is also room for independent citizens' initiatives in Eastern Europe. These things are themselves the fruit of the tendencies towards an understanding both at the international and domestic levels. Their very existence – something that would have been unthinkable in Stalin's time – is a sign of changed circumstances. Despite all their limitations and imperfections, they are a stimulus to further positive changes, especially because they get the authorities used to the existence of elements of independent activity in society. They are persecuted precisely to the extent that the ruling circles feel threatened in their efforts to maintain the internal status quo in uncertain international conditions. Their aim cannot be to seek a confrontation with the authorities, to attempt an overthrow, or to transfer any country from one alliance to the other. Their aim is to establish a dialogue between all social layers and groups, with the idea of finding the best possible solution to social problems.

They cannot, however, adopt the confrontationist stance taken by the authorities, but must persist in the search for a real dialogue. Anybody who longs for revolution, street battles and disturbances should understand that the logic of the blocs rules out that sort of thing. Anybody who wanted, even by peaceful means, to bring about a one-sided revision of the existing arrangements is equally out of touch. The Helsinki Agreements implied a significant step towards the renewal of a traditional understanding of the concept of state sovereignty. But as long as we remain within the confines of the logic of the blocs, then it is to be expected that one-sided threats against the other will be subject to the full force of this logic – even if only from feelings of fear.

On the basis of this understanding we must fight together from San Francisco to Vladivostok to reverse this logic. It is my belief that this means the recognition of certain facts by the European nations:

No one should propose the revision of European borders. In fact, it is necessary openly and publicly to adhere to the principle of their inviolability. At the same time this requires that members of the larger nations should demand equality and the possibility of the fullest development for the smaller nations. In the process of European *rapprochement*, state borders will tend to become nothing more than imaginary lines similar to those which demarcate districts of departments. This process is already taking place between some West European states.

Armament is never justified. It is not possible to demand a one-sided disarmament, or measures of disarmament, only from one's own government. The demand must be placed on all European governments simultaneously. Nor must the argument be used that somebody else's armament is justified by the armament of one's own government. Naturally, it is also unacceptable to condemn only the escalations of another government while remaining silent about the escalations in one's own country or bloc.

It is necessary to demand the removal of all foreign armies from the territory of the European states and the dissolution of NATO and the Warsaw Pact, at first, at the least, through the limitation and withdrawal of their troops.

It is necessary to recognize the right of the Germans to re-unification inside the present borders of Germany, by methods, forms, conditions and under terms which are agreed by the Germans themselves, with the agreement of both super-powers and of all the other European nations. Given the complex of problems surrounding this development, it can only take place as part of a wider process of European *rapprochement.* A non-nuclear and neutralized zone could be created through a series of steps, insofar as they could be agreed upon as phases of a gradual dismantling of the blocs. The form of the new German state might be that of a federation or confederation. The removal of confrontation between the blocs would also eliminate a whole number of points of friction between the two systems which would, in the new conditions, and with the removal from predominance of military concerns, each develop far more freely.

It is necessary to defend consistently the principle of non-intervention, which is set down in all the most important international documents, such as the U N Charter and the Helsinki Accords. *Non-intervention between states must be distinguished from the right to free and open discussion between peoples.* While on the one hand states must stick to the principle that the internal arrangements and conditions inside states are exclusively the concern of the inhabitants of that country, on the other hand citizens must have the right to ask questions freely, and debate, support or criticize those conditions or arrangements. States are specialized institutions, while humanity is only one.

History is and always was a human creation. The conditions in which we live are the creation of the wisdom and stupidity of our forebears. It is up to us, whether we are happy with things as they are and continue to allow history to be made by others, or whether we try to create a world which conforms to our own longings and wishes. Without illusions. A short time from the historical point of view can be a long time from the point of view of one life. None the less, history remains open.

PART FOUR

Making Peace

Back in 1983, when President Reagan first announced his 'vision of hope for the future', we took it to be the optical illusion of an ageing man. To envisage the machinery of Star Wars actually placed in space was tantamount to seeing real shapes in clouds: 'dragonish' clouds maybe, in which we might discern signs of 'black vesper's pageants',* but still, only symbolically as it were. It had to be a mockery of what could happen in reality.

The contradictory aspiration to render militarism obsolete by recourse to militarism remains – as it always will do – fantastical. Yet the 'vision' itself has not dissolved away but rather gains in distinctness even as we watch and wait. Not only in the USA, but here in Britain, too – and the pattern is being repeated elsewhere in Western Europe – it daily acquires more substance. Business as usual has already come to mean Star Wars business. Clandestine research agreements, haggles over funding and the scope of American surveillance, secret contract negotiations: these are now almost routine aspects of scientific and technological activity. Political discussion has immediately followed suit; prompt to familiarize itself with the SDI idiom, it has adjusted with alarming rapidity to this monstrous new arrangement. Reagan's delirious whim, in being indulged, has also been

---

* Sometimes we see a cloud that's dragonish;
  A vapour sometime like a bear or lion,
  A tower'd citadel, a pendant rock,
  A forked mountain, or blue promontory
  With trees upon't, that nod unto the world
  And mock our eyes with air: thou hast seen these signs;
  They are black vesper's pageants.
  Shakespeare, *Antony and Cleopatra*

made sanitary and reprocessed as rationality, thanks to its comforting association with ordinary people and their ordinary goings on in the common rooms of Heriot-Watt or the canteens of Plessey and British Aerospace. 'What am I working on? – Fibre optics, well, yes, part of the S D I programme – want another coffee?'

Let us call this the military manufacture of reality – a process which, did it not work by undermining our powers of disbelief, ought to astonish us greatly. For consider: a U S administration is preparing to sink each year a sum equivalent to the New Zealand G N P in a project as bizarre in its philosophy as it is technically unworkable. The ultimate idea behind it, so it would appear, is to permit all U S aggression to remain immune to its own effects – in other words, to render hatred inviolate; the means to this end is an unearthly apparatus whose complexity bumps up against the limits of scientific conceptualization.

Consider further, that all this is already being implemented in the name of our defence by the combined powers of the N A T O alliance, and not only with the – no doubt predictable – connivance of the present British government, but with no very fearsome roars as yet from the Opposition. As I write, there has been one debate on S D I in the House of Commons (the record of the House of Lords has been rather better) – and this debate took place only *after* the signing of the Memorandum of Understanding, only *after* Lt.-Gen. Abrahamson, the Star Wars chief, had come and gone, British S D I participation a more or less guaranteed eventuality. In the end, however, parliamentary opposition is seldom more noisy than it needs to be. Perhaps we have to infer from all this that Star Wars is going ahead with the compliance of the vast majority of British citizens?

But if this is so, then we should realize what we are up to. For to encourage this folly either by deed or word, or simply by failure to protest (which in these matters amounts to tacit consent), is to assist a nightmare to come true. Defensive mirrors in space are not the phantoms of a troubled conscience they might once have seemed; they are not simply the metaphors of an astral looking-glass world from whose disquieting dream we shall shortly awaken. If we stand idly by, they will most certainly be installed. And the Soviet mirrors will most likely be erected in their image, and glint evilly back at them – until sooner or later, one or other of their imperial architects, in fury at the reflection of its own unblinking gaze, will put through a fistful of ballistic missiles, and the whole extraordinary edifice will shatter in fragments over a burning world.

Yet there is a silver lining of sorts to be found even in this clouded vision, and it lies in the very swiftness with which its crazed imagining has been converted into concrete materiality. For if the so-called 'military–industrial' complex, and its many advocates and lackeys, can wreak such major changes upon reality so suddenly, then may there not be reversals equally dramatic and equally rapid in our toleration of the alterations it effects?

It is true that this would involve the kind of quantum leap in attitude for which there would seem to be no precedents in history. Yet the emergency we now confront is also without historical precedent and there can be no certain prediction that it will not summon forth an equally exceptional struggle to surmount it. Indeed, the vast and growing peace movement is a very evident sign of its beginning to do so. What is undeniable, however, is the necessity of a deeper and much more widespread concern for the present crisis than has yet been felt, and the emergence of much greater public faith in the possibility of nuclear disarmament.

If this is to come about then a very prevalent complacency about the arms race must be disturbed. People will have to stop thinking of it as a kind of permanent bad weather to which they have no choice but to adapt. They will have to review their own adjustment to it and to the onus it now places on each succeeding generation, on individuals who are expected in their passage to adulthood to accustom themselves not only to the fact of individual mortality but to a prospect outside the range of previous human experience: the possible violent death in their lifetime of their species

and all its works. They must question their society's acceptance of this prospect as if it were a henceforth inescapable
feature of the human condition, and work to restore a sense
of outrage that all life should be lived under this shadow. By
whatever means available to them, they must try to restore
faith in the powers of humanity to turn round and come out
from its nuclear cul-de-sac.

For the arms race is not an inevitable blight of nature, but
a humanly contrived disablement. And as such it ought to
inspire, not resignation, but fury. Why, after all, should our
chances of survival and happiness be constantly sacrificed to
something within our powers to alter? Supposing we were to
reverse this process, reinstate the moment of 'pre-nuclear
innocence' and throw off this unremitting restraint on human
well-being?

We should encourage this anger and its storming and
railing at our present handicap; and we should indulge in the
imagining of alternatives which in part provokes it. For the
more desire we generate for a demilitarized world, the more
likely we shall be to enjoy it. We too, then, should begin to
have visions: visions of life in a disarmed society. But if one
aspect of this enterprise is 'Utopian' projection, the other
must be realistic scrutiny of our present acts and attitudes. It
has to be recognized that peace canot be achieved simply by
protesting against various items of military hardware. We
have to tackle the processes which sustain the arms race and
are used to justify its continuance – and these include habits
and expectations of which we may be scarcely conscious, and
whose military consequences we certainly do not intend.

In the first instance, however, we should ask ourselves a
quite straightforward question: why the arms race, what is
its purpose? There are those (Mrs Thatcher, for example)
who will tell us that the arms race must continue because we
know how to make nuclear weapons. But they do not explain
how this knowledge can be made responsible for their production in numbers sufficient to end all human life; nor do
they explain why we are not more given to eating each other,

since we know perfectly well how to do so. Let us turn, then, to what may seem a more promising line of explanation: the arms race is there because it keeps the peace. But do any of us seriously believe that the prospect of the Third World War recedes as the nuclear megatonnage mounts up? If we cast our minds, not over the next decade or two, but over a hundred, two hundred years, then we must surely acknowledge that this frenetic accumulation cannot continue for ever, and there are really only two options facing us: extermination or an end to Cold War and the relentless amassing of arms that goes with it.

For the arms race, in fact, is neither the inevitable consequence of technical know-how, nor is it about avoiding war. What drives it is animosity – an animosity, moreover, which derives at least a part of its force from the existence of the weapons which it supposedly justifies: the fact that it is upon 'us' that the 'enemy's' weapons are targeted in part explains – and quite reasonably so – the hostility that we direct towards the 'enemy'. Yet this, of course, cannot be the whole story, for it begs the question as to what it is that allows this enmity to gain ground in the first place and to hold us all so powerfully in its sway that it could now sweep us all to our deaths in a half hour. The answer to this question is not easy. On the one hand, we want to say that it has no obvious rationale, and that there is little in the history and culture of Europe, and even less in our personal feelings towards the individuals who collectively comprise the 'enemy', that can explain or justify it. Italian bricklayers almost certainly do not want to annihilate Hungarian carpenters, British dancers bear no grudge against their Soviet counterparts, Polish nurses do not want to fry Belgian children; at one level, none of us wants to blow up any of the others at all. On the other hand, we have to face the truth that we are also members of societies that have girded themselves to take the kind of action whose consequences for each of us personally will be precisely of this character. In this sense then, we are also collectively held in thrall to a consuming hatred of the 'enemy', even as we disown any individual animosity.

That people can countenance this situation, and in the process even lend themselves with enthusiasm to an over-arching nationalist or 'public' aggression, is no doubt in part explained by a desire for the sort of self-identity that membership of an 'exclusive' grouping can satisfy, and by the uplifting feelings of solidarity and camaraderie that go along with such forms of belonging. And it is precisely this desire which nationalism or religious or racial fanaticism is able to play upon – often to such terrible effect. No one needs reminding of the kind of irrationally ferocious col-lectivities that have been massaged into existence under these stimuli.

Appalling, however, as the results of these inflated aggres-sions have been in the past, they have never until now been able to draw on the sort of military hardware that is now available to them in such abundance. This means that we face today a situation in which the very survival of life on earth depends on our capacity to make a decisive shift in the affective 'field' of these passions – away from the pole of the aggressive impulses towards those of compassion. The aim must be to resist all those pressures and forms of manipu-lation that encourage us into a hostility that as private indi-viduals we seldom ever really feel, while at the same time fostering all that more personal part of our being that em-pathizes with the 'enemy' plight, can find no reason to slaughter its individual members and recoils from the pros-pect of doing so. When the peace movement calls for a 'people's detente' it is precisely calling for this kind of shift of perceptions. It is saying that the Achilles heel of Cold War antagonism lies in the ability of the individual to transgress the artificial boundaries between nations and peoples that are so assiduously and so destructively sustained at governmental level, and to go talking and walking or kicking balls or making music together in the common 'human' space that lies beyond them.

The capacity for such transgressions depends in part on the extent to which people can credit themselves with pos-session of more complex feelings towards the 'enemy' than the simplistic jingoism of the minority is prepared to allow them. It depends, for example, on a readiness to acknowledge that they overall felt gladder about the contest on the football field in Mexico City – when England was defeated by Argentina in the 1986 World Cup – than about the battle of Goose Green, even as they appreciated, wrily, sadly, angrily or bemusedly the parallels between the two.

But what is at issue here is not simply our ability to go trespassing on the grass together beyond the state-drawn borders, but our moral duty to do so at the present time. For just as government-planned genocide has in the past been assisted on its way simply by citizen default, it is likely to be so again unless sufficient numbers of us are prepared to reach out for an alternative, to seize the initiative from government and to protest 'but the emperor has no clothes: there is no reason to arm ourselves'.[1] To switch the dramatic reference: we Europeans could do with some of the spirit of Dikaiopolis, the 'honest Joe citizen' in Aristophanes' play, *The Archarnians*, who, in frustration at the repeated failure of the Athenian and Spartan governments to agree to any peace formula,[2] makes his personal treaty with the 'enemy' – and thereafter enjoys a private peace and plenty that becomes the envy of the state warmongers.

We can be encouraged, moreover, in such moves by consideration of the fact that it is now the Cold War itself, rather than any enemy as such, which poses the major threat. For in generating ever more substantial national and international frictions, it creates its own 'logic' for the hot war towards which it is tending. The East – West division may have had its origin in the oppositional economic systems of capitalism and Communism, and this may remain in part its justification. But in that case we should recognize how paradoxical it is that East – West trade and economic cooperation has continued however icy the political climate has become. We should recognize, that is, the extent to which Cold War rhetoric has clung to the 'two-systems' idea simply for reasons of militarism itself, and that in this process the more pronounced evils of both systems have been continuously reinforced. In a situation where each side has sought to deny that there could be anything even potentially attractive about the other's way of doing things in order to justify a persisting hostility, inequality and class division in the West have conspired with repression in the East to reproduce the worst abuses of both. An enmity whose official 'causes' could in principle be removed by changes in both systems thus militates against such changes – and in doing so, of course, sustains itself. The Cold War, in other words, depends on a constant projection on the part of the antagonists of their own major shortcomings, the social inequalities associated with capitalist market freedoms being defended as part of the necessary bulwark against Soviet totalitarianism, and the latter being justified by reference to the social divisiveness supposedly entailed by any more liberal policy. In this process the emancipatory elements of both liberal and socialist philosophies are denied, and all impulses to their achievement repeatedly repelled. As unemployment and poverty in the West condemn more and more people to circumstances of existence which either numb the will to change or else divert it into violent and self-destructive paths, the lack of proper channels of political expression in the East induces a mirroring of this nihilism in the cycle of rebellion, repression and disillusionment. In Handsworth, the youth go on the rampage. In Warsaw, authorities inform us that young people have lost their zest for life.[3]

Let us acknowledge, therefore, that the Cold War not only aggravates the worst features of both systems but also inhibits the realization of those aspects to which they respectively appeal in ideological self-defence. For the militarism and repressive apparatus of Soviet-style socialism has relied upon, and continuously reproduced, hierarchies and inequalities of power and income, just as the aggressive defence of Western 'freedom' has issued in oppressive measures of 'law and order' enforcement and seriously eroded democracy. And nowhere is this more pronounced than in matters of defence. Today, in East *and* West, decisions which will ultimately determine the destiny of the collective citizens of

Europe (and indeed of the world at large) are made by olig-
archies – by the Kremlin potentates there, by the NATO
High Level Group here.

The persistent questioning of Cold War psychology and
its sinister indoctrination is, then, the first priority, for it is
the East–West ideological confrontation that poses the most
immediate danger. At the same time, however, we must acknowledge the more long-term threat to global survival which
lies in the North–South division and is perpetuated by the
relentless economic expansionism of the First World nations.
Here, too, individuals have responsibilities to the future
which need to be thought through, in the first instance, by
consideration of the link between affluence and war. For it
is the spiralling competition for the dwindling resources
essential to maintain – and advance – First World living
standards that spurs on the military stockpiling that
heightens the risk of nuclear confrontation. The USA accounts for around 80 per cent of world oil consumption – a
room-sized tank per capita per annum. A domestic pet in
the UK commands many times the purchasing power of a
Sudanese peasant. These facts testify to a century and a
half (at least) of aggressively imperialist consumption which
is as unfair in its consequences for the Third World peoples
now as it is careless of the resource needs of future generations. As part of this same destructive process, dis-
crepancies of privilege within the First World itself have
been accentuated, existing class divisions have been continuously re-confirmed, and the political sovereignty of the
West European nations has been ever more jeopardized by
their reliance on American capital and hence subsumption
to its whim.

None of this need be, however. As Lucio Magri has argued,
Western Europe possesses now, as it did not thirty years ago,
the economic, technological and cultural means to assert its
own political autonomy, and to help sustain another path of
development for the Third World. But, as he also says, the
condition of this would be

... reorientation of the European economies away from the quantitative multiplication of goods for consumption and export and the wastage of natural resources that goes with it, towards another style of development: one that was sober in its consumption, exported technology rather than commodities, sought a reduction in labour-time performed, gave priority to improvements in the quality of living. Such a model of development would no longer find its centre of gravity in heavy technology and industrial concentration, but in decentralized production and communication systems. It would be based not on the expropriation of nature, but on its reconstruction and valorization.[4]

To pursue this route would not be to cast off into a world without joy. The aim is not deprivation but a different balance of gratification: to become abstemious in the consumption of material commodities, but more profligate to compensate in the so-called 'goods of the spirit'. Community, friendship, sexual love, conviviality, wild space, music, theatre, reading and conversation, fresh air and uncontaminated land and water: it is with these attractions we should be cultivating desire and pandering to the senses, rather than with images of improving shares, the flight to the Bahamas and the second car. We should aspire to a new eroticism of consumption, an altered aesthetic of needs: one which makes the senses recoil from commodities which waste the land, throw up ugly environments, pollute the atmosphere, absorb large quantities of energy and leave a debris of junk in their wake.

These commodities are not without their uses, nor do we need to dispense with them altogether. The point, rather, is that they should be 'compromised'. We need to begin to pit their negative qualities against their more positive attributes, and thus little by little complicate a former more spontaneous urge to make use of them. As we watch the Nissan or Range Rover disappearing into a TV sunset at the desert's edge, or gliding noiselessly through leafy English lanes, we should recall that what these vehicles much more typically do is trap us in the din and stench of urban traffic jams, bring cuts in much less wasteful public transport (especially through leafy lanes), and depend on non-renewable oil supplies continuing to flow in from highly militarized and volatile areas of the globe.

To commit ourselves to alternative 'sober consumption' policies on standard facilities such as road transport, air freight, domestic appliances, and the like, would be to open the way to a lifestyle very different from that of the industrialized nations at present. But it would be nowhere like as primitive, arduous or tedious as dismissive modernist critics of all green projections of this kind like to imagine. It is very important, in fact, as a first step to achieving what are, given our present crisis, realist rather than Utopian programmes, that we resist the caricatured versions with which a myopic and self-righteous pragmatism seeks to discredit these conceptions. We are not here mired in romantic nostalgia, nor bent on returning to medieval squalor, ill-health and hard labour. We are suggesting ways of avoiding descent into previously unimagined barbarism and degradation, ending with the extinction of human civilization altogether.

Admittedly, such a programme directly challenges the norms of 'growth' and 'efficiency' which have provided the governing logic of all capitalist economic activity. It also challenges conceptions about work and technology which are common to both capitalist and socialist thinking, and which have long dictated our attitudes to time expenditure. Dominated as our culture is by the idea that all time is better saved than spent, it knows no other way to define the 'efficiency' of its economy except in terms of its labour-saving capacities, and no other way to gauge its technical progress than in terms of its economic 'efficiency'. While the capitalist nations regard any improvement in the time–product ratio as a means to keep down wage bills, thus enhancing profits, the socialist regimes are no less keen on it because of what it permits in the way of promoting the 'capitalist' lifestyle, upon whose provision they believe their legitimation largely depends. The overall result, in both instances, is recourse to technologies aimed at short-term growth rather than long-term reproduction, and designed, not so much to diversify or improve the quality of work, but to curtail its duration.

Of course, labour-saving technologies can in principle help us to spend time in happier ways. In practice, however, the commitment to growth traps us in a Hobson's choice between wasting free time and denying it. If we are not to 'squander' it in the form of a ghettoized and ever more relatively deprived sector of the unemployed, then we must disallow it: we must put the people back to work. If the people are put back to work on useful products satisfying social needs, preferably paid for out of cancelled arms programmes, then this latter policy is vastly to be preferred. But we should not con ourselves into thinking it an indefinitely rational mode of procedure, given the level of our current technical abilities and the ecological constraints we are now under. More rational by far would be a policy geared to provision of a decent but not extravagant standard of living, based on part-time employment for everyone. This would be consistent not only with enjoyment of genuine leisure but with some quite drastic and arguably very beneficial changes in the conduct of domestic life, the upbringing of children and human relationships. Domestic and nurturing tasks could be shared between both sexes, allowing both a richer experience and more mutual understanding. Domestic work itself could become less constraining and tedious because there would be time and energy to provide ourselves with things and services we currently have no choice but to buy or hire. There would be time to spend on each other, to think and talk, teach and learn, make and create, and simply to be idle. Such a pattern of consumption could transform the quality of city life while giving far more people access to the pleasures of the countryside. Above all, it would be consistent with long-term peace and security.

So far are we from realizing any such alternative at the present time that we are inclined to dismiss the whole idea as fanciful. And yet against it must be set the increasingly surreal feel of those consumer paradises in which a prevailing economic rationality invites us to cocoon the imagination. Coming away from a meeting about this book, I was struck by a page in my newspaper, a page in itself quite typical and unremarkable. (Though the events to which it refers were quickly themselves – again typically perhaps – to seem quite dated.) A good third of it is devoted to an insurance-company advertisement depicting three individuals engrossed in thought. They are pondering the use to which they would put some extra cash were it by chance to come their way. The young housewife yearns for a complete new kitchen, the holiday of a lifetime and her own sailing dinghy; the rising manager dreams of his new car, house extension and speedboat; the elderly man of his retirement cottage, holiday flat in Spain and motor cruiser. 'Like everyone else you have a dream you'd like to come true in the not too distant future . . .', patters on the accompanying copy, as within a few column inches of it U S warships are challenging Colonel Gadafy across the 'death line' in the Gulf of Sirte, threatening a skirmish in the Middle East with, who knows, a brush with a lurking Soviet submarine, a nuclear exchange?

One could go on: the imagined investors perusing their 'capital bonus' figures are in visual range not only of reported eyeball contact between Libyan and U S fighter pilots; should they glance upwards they will be staring into the eyes of a heavily armed National Resistance army guerrilla in Uganda – a country where loft conversions and motor cruisers are not plentiful, and where there has been little of permanence save the steady import of arms and export of coffee. If, pausing for a moment in their calculation of their 'total illustrated maturity value', they cast an eye across the page, they will read of the very premature death of Franscina Legoeete at the hands of the South African police – and also of their government's refusal to impose sanctions on the guilty regime (partly through fear, perhaps, of the impact on British savings investments?).

Enough of this. These prudent citizens are not real people, but put-up jobs screening us from our less one-dimensional selves. Real people do not look or think like these dummies.

They wince at the daily narrative of torture, death and waste. They live in fear of nuclear destruction, are appalled at the sight of starving Third World peasants, and send generous donations to Oxfam. Many of them, all too aware of the fragility of their everyday existence, join the peace movement and become very active within it. And yet real people are also terribly caught up in the concerns and aspirations of consumer shams, even as they seek to distance themselves from the identity which they are offered by them.

This is the dilemma of First World existence: that none of us can escape this other 'utilitarian-consumerist' face or see ourselves as wholly freed of guilt; yet none of us, either, know how to extract ourselves as individuals from the cycle of oppression. Indeed, not only are we so far steeped in this that we doubt whether there *is* a way out; we also, though perhaps less consciously, are fearful that in any change of our ways we might forfeit our identity as well. Yet together with this fear, there also goes deep dissatisfaction and a yearning for something else. We question the worth of life, and wonder whether we are any nearer to happiness than our forebears. We express regret at the loss of a clearly felt but elusive sense of community, and experience the invasion in its place of a sinister brittleness. So that alongside, and even implicit in the hesitations and the feelings of impotence, there would seem to be a longing for a different order of human society – and for the emergence of precisely that solidarity and common sense of purpose which could enable us to overcome our individual powerlessness to achieve it.

It will be objected, however, that so long as the military blocs persist, so long as individuals are deprived of political expression in the East, and Western societies remain so economically divisive, then any appeal to a 'we' of Europe or of the First World to improve the condition of the Third must remain rhetorical. In one sense, this is true: there is certainly, at the moment, no national or international constituency in Europe to which such a 'we' might in all good conscience be applied. And yet in one important sense there is a 'we' – the 'we' that cuts across these other divisions to unite those millions of citizens of the First World countries who feed themselves committed to nuclear disarmament and the building of long-term peace.

The historical significance of the international peace movement in laying the grounds for the emergence of this collectivity should not be underestimated. Given the crucial importance of its work, it is quite scandalous how little encouragement it receives through official political and media channels. Desperately in need of constructive support of that kind, what it daily contends with instead is a barrage of argument designed to convince all those who might otherwise come out more fully in support of it, of the impossibility of any major changes of direction.

It is immensely discouraging to press for such changes and to argue for them on moral grounds in a culture where at every turn one is rebuffed by politicians defending the greater wisdom of pragmatism, economists reminding one of the limited strategic options permitted by the movement of finance capital, or intellectuals wrily deconstructing one's humanist foibles. Moral argument and appeal, these mentors all insist, is either futile or counter-productive. Where it is not ignored, it takes effect only in the form of a resentment which reinforces resistance to its pressure. Since people never change their ways except under the prod of economic necessity, it is pointless for politicians to appeal to any better instinct than immediate financial self-interest. Much sager, then, for them to deal with the electorate like a pack of Pavlovian dogs who only respond with the confirming X if administered a suitable consumerist stimulus.

At the same time, of course, the politicians themselves adopt the same reflex posture towards their own activities and choices, regarding these as permanently under the dictate of economic forces (the 'balance of payment deficit', 'petro-dollar movements', 'sterling rates', etc.) as unassailable in status as the law of gravity. All policy, they never tire of telling us, is a matter of 'manoeuvring' within the narrow constraints imposed by a series of supposedly quite irremovable pressures.

It is this discourse and its realpolitik reminder of the possible effect of an anti-NATO vote on tariff concessions which was used so successfully to sway the Spanish people in the run-up to the 1986 referendum. It is the same language which has been used to persuade the Italians of the need for Comiso (and cuts in public spending), the Dutch of the need for cruise (and cuts in public spending), the British of the need for cruise and Trident, and nuclear power, and the Channel tunnel . . . (and cuts in public spending).

The economic institutions which now mediate practically all international (and much of our inter-personal) exchange are undeniably very powerful and very material forces. But it would be wrong to present them as absolutely beyond all human control, for they exist, in fact, only in virtue of those elements – human will, action, energy, consent, indifference – which together amount to the exercise of such control. The law of gravity will continue to enforce its rule with or without our intervention or our leave. Market forces, NATO, the arms lobby, the Warsaw Pact, Comecon and IMF will not.

An important condition, then, of emancipation from the destructive tendencies of our culture is freedom from a way of thinking which denies the role of people in creating social processes and institutions. It is a way of thinking manifest in many walks of life: the academic preaches it in erudite discourses on the 'death of the subject'; the Cabinet Minister repeats it in voicing fears lest the rise in oil prices will mean more deaths from hypothermia; the citizen who chucks aside the Star Wars leaflet with a derisory snort at the futile struggles of the peace movement is merely acting out its gloomy lesson.

It is an insidious teaching – and in that it induces impotence by convincing us of it, it tends to be self-fulfilling. Yet its picture is none the less distorted. The massive response to the Live Aid and Band Aid appeals indicates that the citizens of the First World are not quite as blinkered or incapable of initiative as the anti-moralists would like us to believe. In sacrificing some part of their savings for the sake of the lives of others whom they will never see, they have shown themselves uneasy with their 'peace' or at any rate distressed by some of its consequences. It remains to be seen how this unease will develop. Certainly, salving conscience with a monetary donation will not be enough. If there is genuine concern to establish a safer and juster world, then people must now put their political voice and energy where they have begun to put their money. They must demand principled political representation of the moral alternatives to which they wish to be committed. Conversely, the onus is on the major European socialist parties to put the 'Pavlovian' theory of the electorate to the test by provision of a strongly argued moral alternative for which it could cast its vote.

In the meanwhile, the peace movement must continue to insist that what is here called the 'moral' option is also the only one that can be credited with realism in a nuclear world. The sheer destructive capacity of modern arsenals – which guarantee that the 'whole' explodes should any 'part' have recourse to nuclear weapons – has rendered anachronistic the conception of the nation state as an autonomous unit with the 'right' to compete with other nations for markets and resources, if necessary protecting the 'vital' interests it thereby establishes by military means. Were, indeed, every nation to adhere to American logic on this 'right' (if the Libyans didn't want the Sixth Fleet in the Gulf of Sirta, they should have asserted their 'right' to it, according to a Pentagon spokesman at the time of Libyan–US clash in April 1986) then the result, as the US administration well knows, would be disaster for everyone. In the last analysis, if the human race is to survive its 'nuclear epoch', it will have to adjust to the political perspective which the technical capacities of its armaments have forced upon it: it must come to accept the world in its entirety as a single body politic of which the separate national units are the various limbs and organs. Henceforth no one 'member' can go it alone without risking dismembering the whole upon which it itself depends for its survival.

To challenge the longstanding idea of the nation state as

the ultimate political grouping is to open up a new conception of the political identity and status of the individual. It is to insist that the interests which individuals have as members of a common species are at odds with the 'nationalistic' interests fostered by the state, and can find no adequate representation in the latter. Individuals, for their part, must seek, as part of this same conception, to replace patriotic and nationalist loyalties by a 'species responsibility' – by a consciousness of the organicity of the planet and of the duties that each person has towards it as part of a collective human subject. For though as individuals we can only engage at any time in particular actions in particular geographical regions, it is these specific and local doings in the aggregate that decide the history and fate of our species taken as a whole. In this sense, as Rudolf Bahro has suggested, human beings are subjects of their history, not only individually but also as a species, and it is only if we refuse to look at the matter in this larger perspective that we can continue to insist that social forces and institutions are autonomous of individuals and unamenable to their control. As he puts it:

> Everything which looms as a danger to human beings [the social ensemble], everything which threatens them or it, is either their own alienated power or is obeying their alienated command. The central control rooms may be lords over death, but they are not lords of the process which put them in this position.[5]

But recognition of a 'species-responsibility' along these lines must itself be grounded in appreciation of the physical and psychological ties uniting all members of the human race and rendering them a species in common. For paradoxical though it may seem, it is through a heightened awareness of those qualities we deem more 'personal' that we are best able to arrive at a sense of ourselves as members of a larger trans-national collectivity. In other words, the assumption of 'global subjectivity' goes together with a shift in values in which those characteristics we share with others in being human are given a much more positive estimation than hitherto, while those we share specifically as British (or American, or Russian or Chinese . . .) are viewed more circumspectly. In this process, as feminist peace campaigning has always rightly insisted, it is crucial that we begin to give their proper due to those 'private' domestic activities which have hitherto always been subordinated to the 'larger' concerns of a 'public' domain – where war, polity and the pursuit of wealth supposedly make trifles of these 'womanly' pursuits. The human race will not survive unless it wakes up to the fact that giving birth, caring for our offspring, and all forms of nursing and ministering to each other, both physically and emotionally, are far more vital to the ultimate well-being and protection of our species than anything we do in the way of military defence.

To give priority in this way to unmediated person-to-person emotional ties and physical dependences is to begin to dismantle that enmity which flourishes on the idea that an entire population can be designated the bloodless and bodiless 'other' of an equally incorporeal, abstracted 'self'. To give ourselves (and our enemies) bodies and minds again, which bleed and caress and love and feel afraid, is immediately to invest ourselves with an important source of power against the degenerative spiral of militarism. For every twist in that spiral is accomplished only with the aid of personnel, both military and civilian, who are prepared and able to refuse identification with the victims of planned aggression.

Militarism works through inculcating a resistance to empathy which is self-reproducing and self-confirming. It is this failure of compassion which encourages the 'nuke 'em' philosophy, makes possible the tolerance of preparations for annihilation, and lies behind the impassive contemplation of the use of nuclear arsenals. In working to check militarism the peace movement is therefore struggling against repression and apathy, and attempting to stop the rot of something even more dangerous than lethargy: the crowing 'Gotcha!' Falklands mentality which cannot for a minute permit itself to identify, not with the 'getter' but the 'got'.

Very few of us are actually able to be so wholly insensitive to the sufferings of others. Yet we should recognize none the less that time is running out, and that militarism kills not only in war and in the massive Third World casualties of the global arms race, but also by a progressive deadening of our emotional responsiveness and energy. Built into the 'exterminist' process, as part of its cancerous advance, there is a mutilation of the affective and moral being, an enfeebling of the will to live and general blunting of our sensibility to the pain and loss of fellow human beings. If we are finally snuffed out by our own doing, it will be this lapse of will and feeling that will be ultimately to blame. The alternative is to fan the flame of human forbearance and magnanimity: to summon up the resolution to survive – and flourish. For there is still much 'capability and god-like reason' left in us, and we should turn it now, not to vengeful deeds, but to those acts of peace which need so urgently to be done. The nuclear shields with which the arms race is currently threatening to eclipse the future are certainly intricate devices, and the product of complex forces. Yet there is nothing we have humanly engineered which is not vulnerable in the end to our refusal to allow it to continue. Against the Goliath of the 'technical fix' we must now pit the David resources of the human spirit.

Notes

1. The image is invoked by the Hungarian writer, Andras Hegedüs in an article printed in *END Journal*, Summer 1986.
2. The play is written and set during the Peloponnesian war between the city-states of Athens and Sparta, which began in 432 BC and lasted nearly thirty years, to the detriment of all parties.
3. The overall conclusion of an official survey of youth attitudes in Poland, reported in the *Guardian*, 10 March 1986, is that hardly anyone under thirty-five cares anything for People's Poland, and that most suffer from a notable 'lack of vigour'.
4. Lucio Magri, 'The peace movement and Europe', in *Exterminism and Cold War*, London, Verso, 1982, p. 132.
5. Rudolf Bahro, *Building the Green Movement*, London, Heretic, 1986, p. 144.

General, your tank is a powerful vehicle
it brings down a forest and crushes a hundred people
but it has a fault
it needs a driver.

General, your bomber plane is powerful
it flies faster than a storm and carries more than an elephant
but it has a fault
it needs a mechanic.

General, people are very useful
they can fly and they can kill.
But they have one fault:
they can think.

Bertolt Brecht, tr. Owen Davies

Throughout this book contributors have referred to 'the peace movement' as if it was one clearly defined national or international organization. But of course there is no such tidy organization, and, beyond the various organized movements, there is a more widely dispersed movement of the spirit and of consciousness which inspires multitudes who may never join organizations or wear the movements' badges.

In any case, the 'peace movement' has its own divisions and its own internal arguments, and is made up of hundreds of smaller movements, each with its own distinctive accents and goals, who join together in some major actions and who share the same broad cause. One way to explain all this is to describe developments in the British peace movement over the last five years – a movement which (through countless meetings and personal discussions) I may know as well as any other person. Yet to describe this one nation's movement is an awe-inspiring task. How can one hope to do justice to a campaign which has involved literally hundreds of thousands of individuals and which has encompassed every conceivable type of group?

'The splitting of the atom has changed everything except our ways of thinking, and thus we drift to unparalleled disaster,' said Einstein. Changing public policy by changing public ways of thinking is the central task of the peace movement in a democratic society, and to do this we need diverse approaches, as diverse as human beings – we all start from different points and it takes entirely different stimuli to jolt each of us into critical appraisal of the accepted ways of thinking about nuclear weapons, deterrence and the whole concept of 'defence' in a world as precariously perched as we are today on the 'edge of darkness'. The greatest achievement of the last five years has been the new critical and informed awareness of millions of people about what was supposed to be secret. The doors have been opened and they are never going to be closed again.

Contrary to government propaganda, I can report that the peace movement, alive and knowledgeable, is no monolith which has hijacked the word 'peace' but is as varied as humanity itself. Just as the oldest peace organizations in this country, such as the National Peace Council, the Quaker peace committee, or the Fellowship of Reconciliation, were in time joined after the First World War by newer initiatives such as the Peace Pledge Union or *Peace News*, so these in turn were joined by groups like CND, responding to the new possibility of nuclear annihilation. Other groups, the Campaign Against the Arms Trade (CAAT), for example, did not arrive until the 1970s, while the peace movement of the 1980s has flowered in many different ways and organizations, all of which have made an indispensable contribution to the task of changing public opinion.

We have, first of all, been expertly served with well-researched publications and information, from the Bradford

School of Peace Studies to A D I U and S I P R I. All the major publishers have offered titles, of fact or fiction, on the nuclear issue, and large audiences were attracted by films such as *Threads, The Day After, Testament,* and the long-overdue television showing of Peter Watkin's 'The War Game'. The activities of local peace groups, particularly with neighbourhood events to mark occasions such as the Hiroshima–Nagasaki commemoration each year, have ensured that the peace issue has never been far from the pages of local newspapers in every district and parish. Door-to-door canvassing, leafleting, street stalls and local radio phone-ins have given us a chance to reach thousands who would never dream of coming to a public meeting, let alone of joining an organization.

A major feature of recent years has been the formation of professional peace groupings of musicians, journalists, farmers, engineers, architects, philosophers and many others. The evidence assembled in a report such as *The Medical Effects of Nuclear War*[1] produced by the British Medical Association's Board of Science and Education, can hardly be called Kremlin propaganda, but it will have given the Home Office little cause for comfort. Deliberately avoiding the possibility of being charged with taking sides in the disarmament debate, the Board concluded:

The N H S could not deal with the casualties that might be expected following the detonation of a single one-megaton weapon over the U K. It follows that multiple nuclear explosions over several, possibly many, cities would force a breakdown in medical services across the country as a whole ... We believe that such a weight of nuclear attack would cause the medical services in the country to collapse.

This verdict confirmed the work done at international level by the International Physicians for the Prevention of Nuclear War, whose efforts were more recently recognized by the Nobel Peace Prize award.

From a similar international coalition of U S and Soviet scientists have come equally damning reports – publicized here by SANA, Scientists Against Nuclear Arms – on the hellish predictions the investigators have termed 'the nuclear winter'. They graphically describe a world, frozen in darkness and decay, which even Dante would have had difficulty imagining, but which subsequent research has only supported.

Enormous interest has also been shown in many practical ways by the trade union movement. The majority of trade unions are now affiliated to CND and many produce excellent educational material on the nuclear arms race and its dangers.

One message, at least, has I think been clearly received and understood: widespread professional and public scepticism that civil defence against nuclear attack has any purpose or value whatsoever. The refusal of many local authorities to cooperate with such preparations, and the public information provided by the nuclear-free-zone local authorities, has had tangible effect in the cancellation the 1982 'Hardrock' civil defence exercise and in the thwarting of other plans.

Lawyers for Nuclear Disarmament have been attempting to convey a somewhat more complex, but equally important message, namely, that nuclear warfare and preparations to wage it are not only dangerous and immoral, but actually *illegal* according to international laws, including the Hague and Geneva Conventions and Protocols which limit the methods of warfare (gas, reprisals, environmental poisoning, large-scale bombardment, etc.) and provide for the protection of neutrals and civilians. Conspiracy to plan and prepare for war and other crimes against humanity violate both the international Nuremberg Principles and our own Genocide Act.

These laws have grave implications, not only for members of the armed forces who are regularly expected to rehearse for nuclear war, but for every adult individual who is paying taxes or who otherwise (even by silence) assents to defence policy based on willingness to commit nuclear mass murder. *The British Manual of Military Law* actually tells servicemen and women specifically that they will not escape liability if they obey orders which 'violate the unchallenged rules of warfare . . .' Thousands of individuals have indicated their *dissent* from illegal policies by taking part in non-violent direct action and by being prepared to get arrested for civil disobedience. Over 10,000 of them have been arrested in the UK and Eire since September 1981 for such actions.[2]

The Quakers in particular have taken up the challenge to conscience posed by the payment of taxes for defence purposes. Persistent individuals have had their property confiscated after repeatedly attempting to withhold the military portion of their taxes, or to divert it to the Overseas Development Ministry or some other cause, while the collective stand taken by staff at Friends House added contemporary meaning to their historic witness to the Quaker Peace Testimony.

Numerous other ordinary folk have quite literally put their bodies where their beliefs were, by physically blocking the progress of war preparations; by successfully halting work on the Bridgend Bunker, even to the moment when the concrete was being poured; by coming in hundreds to be arrested at blockades of the Upper Heyford, Burghfield, Greenham and Molesworth bases, and by maintaining a more permanent vigil by living at the peace camps. The presence of camps at many sites has done much to alert the public to the location and number of American bases on these islands, and to an awareness that we are already, in many respects, a country occupied by a foreign military power.

It is a credit to the integrity, organization and true purpose of members of the peace movements that this intense programme of protest action has been entirely non-violent. Insistence on advance training and the use of 'affinity groups' whose members know one another has nearly always weeded out the unprepared or inadequately motivated.

Once in court, many defendants have referred to the precepts of international law in defence of the 'crimes' against property of which they have been accused, and have acquired a sophisticated grasp of the law themselves. Using international law, a group of Greenham women took the US government to court for the crime of deploying cruise missiles in Europe.

In a defensive position, the forces of 'law and order' have been increasingly manipulative and severe in applying the law against peace activists. Their severity has been shown, for example, in a sentence of twelve months for Ann Francis, a vicar's wife, convicted for damaging the fence at Greenham and in the use of conspiracy laws against the Alconbury nine and the Carmarthen seventeen.

Manipulation has taken the form of devices such as avoidance of charges which would lead to trial before a jury in the crown courts, and has resulted in the erosion of civil liberties, particularly at Greenham, where a combination of by-laws, injunctions and other forms of intimidation have been used to move women from one piece of land after another, to prevent them from using caravans and even tents, to prevent anyone from touching the perimeter fence, to harass them with daily evictions and at different times to stop water supplies, douse camp fires, withhold mail and attempt to deprive them even of voting rights.

In fact, understanding has grown throughout the peace movement that to protect nuclear weapons the political and military establishment will stop at almost nothing. Individuals who have phoned-in comments to radio programmes or written to local papers have been visited by Special Branch officers and had their phones and post interfered with. The surveillance which many suspected was confirmed when Cathy Massiter, a former employee of MI5, bravely revealed that phone-tapping of CND officials, infiltration of the peace movement and other forms of observation had indeed been authorized, and the information collected was used by Mr Heseltine to try and discredit the peace movement during the 1983 election campaign.[3] Behind these official attempts to portray us as well-meaning but naïve, woolly-hatted and woolly-minded, has lurked a scurrilous and altogether dirtier campaign, waged by pressure groups set up specially to counter CND. Tactics have included bringing pressure to bear on people through their work (such as the insinuations made about Joan Ruddock's job with the Citizens' Advice Bureau) and repeated smears implying that the peace movement is paid for by the Kremlin. No challenge to provide evidence for these accusations has been met, but mud, once thrown, is inclined to stick. As late as 1985, over a hundred Conservative Members of Parliament were prepared to sign an Early Day Motion which claimed that CND had received £6m from the Russians in 1981.

Lack of evidence has also been a marked feature of the vigorous operation led by a small but vocal band of opponents against the spread of peace studies in schools and colleges, asserting that the subject is a cover for 'Marxist penetration in the classroom', for pacifist propaganda and brainwashing children in favour of 'one-sided disarmament'. In its document, *Education for Peace*, the National Union of Teachers deplored these 'attempts to disrupt proper professional approaches to peace education by imputing political motives to professionals involved in curriculum development'. It recognized that 'interest has evolved from a heightened public concern about international tension and the escalation of the arms race and from teachers' concern to respond in an appropriate and professional manner to the anxieties expressed by pupils', and pointed out:

The Government recognized the need for pupils to be acquainted with the problems of arms control and disarmament when it endorsed the following statement:

'With a view to contributing to a greater understanding and awareness of the problem created by the armaments race and of the need for disarmament, governments and governmental and non-governmental international organizations are urged to take steps to develop programmes of education for disarmament and peace studies at all levels.'

(First United Nations Special Session on Disarmament, New York, 1978, Clause 106)[4]

But both in theory and practice, no one has ever suggested that peace education should be confined to the disarmament issue. It must explore also

the existence of conflict between people, and within and between nations. It investigates the causes of conflict and violence embedded within the perceptions, values and attitudes of individuals, as well as within the social, political and economic structures of society, and encourages the search for alternatives, including non-violent solutions, and the development of skills necessary for their implementation.[5]

As one of the pioneers in this field, Atlantic College, has put it, peace studies is not a 'new' subject, but an attempt to apply insights and information from various fields of knowledge to the foremost problem of our day, and the need for such analysis and understanding seems to me self-evident.

It is self-evident, too, to the generation of young people who feel their lives threatened. The active ones have joined Youth CND and started their own organizations like Schools Against the Bomb. The passive ones, in classroom after classroom, express their sense of powerlessness, their firm belief that annihilation will overtake the world, shortening their lives, and casting shadows of uncertainty and apathy over any purpose in working for exams, a job (if they can get one) or any kind of future. It surprises me that the pessimism of the young, and the long-term effect on the psychological mood of this country, is not causing greater concern.

Inter-disciplinary awareness – the making of connections – has been on the other hand one of the most hopeful signs in the peace movement of the 1980s, and one of the most fruitful of these has been the feminist connection. A catalyst has been the women's peace camp at Greenham Common, a beacon of resistance to cruise missiles, as the women there have maintained continuous vigil, through snow, storm, harassment and extreme vilification. Since the arrival of cruise, their practical purpose of keeping watch has enabled the wider Cruisewatch network to track every exercise of the cruise convoys, mostly moving at night, indicating just how unacceptable their presence is on British soil.

But the all-women camp has inspired women, nationally and internationally, to channel their anger, anxiety and disaffection from war-fighting plans, by becoming confident and active in areas where they were hitherto largely absent. By tradition they were expected to leave political, military and legal matters to men. The empowerment of women is visible in peace groups all over the country, and Greenham has done us all a service by making clear connections between domestic and international violence, cultural acceptance of male dominance and therefore of a culture of political aggression. In the words of an American, Sister Joan Chittister,

Half of the people of the world are going to be exterminated by the nuclear wars that men are designing to protect them – and nobody's even going to ask us if that's alright.[6]

CND wisely remains a single-issue campaign, but its efforts to strengthen the various links demonstrate its understanding that reliance on nuclear weapons is held in place by a web of connected issues. One such connection that has to be made is the financial one – that expenditure on military research, development and production – the £11,000 m projected purchase of Trident for example – has a direct bearing on the resources available for social services. 'The cuts' cannot be fought in isolation, nor can unemployment. CND has sponsored research into alternative employment possibilities for Barrow shipyard workers where Trident is to be constructed.

Our efforts to expose the radiation hazard of nuclear weapons and the transport of warheads between Burghfield and Coulport go hand in hand with the creativity of Greenpeace and Friends of the Earth in publicizing the deceptive practices of the nuclear-power industry in its attempt to hide the dangers of pollution at Sellafield and of the transport of nuclear waste through densely populated areas. All these issues have in turn heightened awareness in Britain of the international dimension. New Zealand's initiative in refusing to allow nuclear-armed warships into its ports, despite massive American pressure, has given individuals, peace organizations and political parties around the world courage and determination.

We have been stirred by visitors and news coverage reporting the pitiful plight of the Pacific Islanders whose way of life, food, children, have been dealt a death-blow by nuclear tests in the area since 1946. We have been awakened to the injustices suffered by the British and American servicemen, now cancer victims but uncompensated, who were told to shut their eyes and turn their backs when they were used as radiation guinea-pigs at nuclear test sites in the Pacific, the US and Australia in the fifties. Most of all, in recent years, the public has been roused to generous action by the sight of starvation in Ethiopia. This has brought home the North–South divide and raised interest in the disarmament–development connection as nothing has done before, despite the urgent concern of the Brandt and Palme Commission reports.

The slogan *Bread not Bombs* has become very much more than a slogan. Its message is being understood and it is motivating thousands. Much more open connections are being made between world poverty and world militarism by the British Oversea Aid agencies, especially Oxfam and War on Want. People are realizing that to talk about poverty at home or abroad without dealing with the vast drain of resources and of talent which a greedy arms race demands is just not possible.

Locally and nationally, the North–South link has been matched by a realization that future international security will also have to be based on improved East–West relations, rather than on the Cold War rhetoric of recent years. END in particular has made a speciality of linking up with forces working for peace in East European countries, while small delegations of all descriptions, of mothers, churches, civic officials, and so on, have visited Communist countries in formal and informal capacity to see for themselves rather than accept the given propaganda.

The alliance of peace movements working round the globe for the same goals has been cooperative and productive. It has shown that millions of ordinary citizens are prepared to go on to the streets to demonstrate for peace. Nearly a million marched in New York alone in a fervent appeal to the governments of the world when they gathered for the United Nations Second Special Session on Disarmament in June 1982. But as speaker after speaker rose in the UN Assembly, it became clear that very few governments had the slighest intention of putting meaning into their words by taking any effective disarmament action. The results in Geneva have been no better, where for the most part negotiations seem to have ground to a halt.

So alongside the good news I have been giving about the growth and vigour of a peace movement which has made real progress in terms of public education on the issues, the bad news is that we are like David pitted against the Goliath of the combined force of the politico-military-industrial interests which maintain the relentless dynamic of the arms race. There is still a long way to go before this dynamic is thrown into reverse.

Valuable opportunities have been missed. I am thinking not only of the Special Session on Disarmament, but also of the long list of proposals from all sorts of sources which could have been effective if the political will had existed.

What about the suggestion by George Kennan (US Ambassador to the USSR 1952/3) that the US and the USSR could make a 50 per cent cut in their nuclear arsenals and still have plenty to negotiate about? (1981)[7]

What of the recommendation of the UN Expert Group on the Relationship Between Disarmament and Development (chaired by Ing Thorsson) that there should be an international Disarmament Fund for Development established by the UN to channel money from arms to human need? (1981)[8]

What about the proposal for a battlefield nuclear-weapon-free zone and a chemical-weapon-free zone, spreading outwards from the centre of Europe, as suggested in the report of the Palme Commission, *Common Security: A Programme for Disarmament*, along with numerous other constructive ideas to build up mutual trust? (1982)[9]

What of the realistic non-nuclear options for Britain outlined by the Alternative Defence Commission in its report, *Defence Without the Bomb?* (1983)[10]

What about the appeal made by India, Argentina, Mexico, Sweden, Greece and Tanzania, that the nuclear nations should freeze the testing, production and deployment of nuclear weapons to allow space for renewed talks about reducing nuclear stockpiles altogether? (1984)[11]

What about Mr Gorbachov's unilateral nuclear test ban, so derisively flouted by the United States and Britain?[12]

These and many other initiatives have been greeted by a deafening silence – particularly by the British government, whose role in international negotiations on arms reduction has been wilfully obstructive, and whose contribution to any measure of multilateral disarmament has been almost non-existent.

Yet this record has hardly been questioned by the opposition parties, even during the 1983 election campaign when so much was being made by the Conservatives of Labour's policy of 'one-sided disarmament'. Repeated use of this phrase, the deliberate suggestion that what we are really seeking is the unilateral disarmament of the West and full exploitation of a falsely drawn division between 'unilateral' and 'multilateral' disarmament has left a legacy of confusion in the public mind – and language – which I'm afraid we have still to rectify. In the Annual Report of the National Peace Council for 1981, Sheila Oakes neatly explained the problem:

In Britain a lot of play has been made by the government on the alleged difference between unilateral and multilateral disarmament, and we should not allow ourselves to be either diverted or divided. Every decision for a new weapon is unilateral. Every decision not to have a new weapon is unilateral. When several governments agree to the same action unilaterally they make a treaty, and invite other governments to agree, unilaterally, to sign it. The atmospheric test ban in 1963 came about in this fashion. There was no agreed treaty to allow the deployment of cruise or Pershing II, or indeed, the SS-20, but apparently it requires a treaty to stop or remove them.[13]

'Unilateral' has been made such a dirty word in Britain

that most people take a lot of convincing that it is a perfectly respectable concept, approved by the majority of the United Nations, and the subject of an important but ignored report of the Secretary-General of the UN in 1984, *Unilateral Nuclear Disarmament Measures*. It is the complete reversal of our government's position:

Important bilateral talks between the two major powers remain suspended, while multilateral efforts, though continuing, are not producing tangible results. In this context unilateral initiatives acquire particular urgency and potential and deserve close scrutiny ... There is no either/or choice between unilateral and negotiated measures of disarmament. Both are needed in view of their complementary nature.

This deliberately fostered confusion shows up in the surveys which reveal that while public opposition can be mounted to particular new weapons systems, public opinion is still convinced that Britain will be left vulnerable without nuclear weapons. 'If they've got them, we must have them' is still a firmly held belief, and the misleading notion of 'balance' still holds sway. What can balance and parity mean in a world where we can already kill each other *so* many times over?

In my travels round the country, addressing public meetings at least five, and often more, times a week, the same underlying anxieties can be detected. Chief among these persists the fear that the Russians are intent on invading the West, and that any peace initiative from Moscow cannot be trusted, because they are militarily 'stronger' and are only seeking to take advantage. The only change in this scenario about who is the 'enemy' is that Colonel Gadafy gets mentioned more often now as a possible source of trouble because it is thought that he is mad enough to start a nuclear war in person.

Widespread ignorance remains and the penny still hasn't dropped about a number of key concepts: that nuclear weapons are so dangerous that we're safer without them; that British ones are not 'independent', that they make us a target and serve no purpose other than suicide; that things are not static – proliferation is a reality and a danger; that plenty of non-nuclear avenues could be explored; that if Soviet peace gestures are a bluff, we lose nothing and might gain something by responding for a given period and calling that bluff.

The fact that ignorance and fear prevail is hardly surprising, so deep-rooted is the primary faith of our fellow citizens in nationalism and militarism. If you thought things were changing you have only to remember what happened during the Falklands war when we saw just how deep lies that nationalism, raw and primitive, ready to be roused as soon as an 'enemy' is located. The service of the nation can demand anything of its subjects, and will excuse any amount of falsehood and deception. Do not forget the *Belgrano*!

The idol of nationalism is worshipped alongside the idol of militarism: the unshakeable belief that violent and military means are really the only/viable/best/strong/manly way of getting through a conflict, even if other ways exist. ('We won the war after all. What would you have done in 1939?') These idols are revered throughout our culture and we make sure in a thousand ways, both blatant and hidden, that our children receive the same faith. The whole weight of the message received through the media is measured in its favour. For this reason I am bemused when I am asked to give the final lecture in a term's series at a public school, or to make up the fourth member of a radio or discussion panel 'to add balance' to what the organizers obviously believe to be an unbiased programme!

I'm afraid that the media – though there have been some fair reporting and some worthwhile programmes – have been especially culpable. As we know, political considerations have prevented some television programmes from being screened, but more insidious has been the more or less continuous distortion by some sections of the media which has only fed popular fear, ignorance, nationalism and militarism. One has been aware throughout the past six years of a hidden policy about what is the acceptable news story of the moment. In 1980 it took the media quite a few months to catch up with the fact that CND was still alive, let alone active and expanding. For about two years this was an acceptable story. Then there was evidently a decision to staunch the flow of programmes on the nuclear issue. As I write I notice that the fashion has now changed once again. The current version of the truth, everywhere it seems except the *Guardian*, is that the peace movement is finished. 'It's finished, folks' is what will from now on be reported, whatever else might happen.

This is an over-simplified account, I know, and the role of the media in the nuclear debate, Nukespeak, has been properly documented elsewhere. But the effect is control and manipulation, so that news stories which don't conform to the accepted image of the peace movement do not appear. For example, CND always deplored the deployment of Soviet SS-20 missiles along with cruise and Pershing II. But this did not register. A very successful CND event took place in July 1983, when a continuous chain of people linked the US and Soviet Embassies in London, and letters were handed into both. This event was hardly reported at all. Thus the message that has been seen and heard is that CND is pro-Soviet and anti-American.

The people I meet around the country – largely innocent of the fact that the press is manipulated even in a society as comparatively free as Britain's – commonly suppose that they, ordinary people, can do nothing about the situation themselves. Both young and old feel impotent, think that the issues are too complex and that they can have no real influence on decisions taken elsewhere by other people. The idea that politicians know best has been shaken by the performance of President Reagan with his inept interference in the affairs of other parts of the globe. However, this too only reinforces the general apathy and disaffection from the complex mystique of politics which politicians encourage at their peril when they ride roughshod over democratically expressed and widely held opinion.

Those of us in the peace movement have a lot of work ahead if we are to overcome this sense of frustration and powerlessness and convince even more people in the mainstream of public opinion of the truth and sanity of our case. Time is on our side in one sense – that as dissatisfaction grows in this country, people who have been on the sidelines will be drawn into making choices. One hopes this will include the leadership of the Church of England for example, who, despite *The Church and the Bomb* and similar discussions, have managed to avoid coming off the fence on the specific issues which the country has faced on the nuclear-weapon deployments of recent years. In this they are not alone. The Roman Catholic church in England and Wales (but certainly not in Scotland) has shown equal timidity. But hope has come from the smaller churches and, of course, from the Society of Friends.

The realist must acknowledge, however, that time is against us. We must build now on the current strength of the peace movement to work more closely still with all our colleagues in the international network and to encourage all the links which will reach others – North–South, East–West, feminist, green, youth, trade union, Christian and so on. These are not diversions, but insights crucial to our understanding of the nuclear threat and our ability to combat it.

The challenge before us, in the time that is left, is to turn informed indignation into the power of political change. In the British political world, where the two- or three-party system effectively prevails, there are special difficulties. It is essential that a government comes to power in Britain with a genuine concern for social justice and the resolve to put an end to the arms race. That has to mean either a Labour government or a coalition involving the Labour Party as the major partner.

Peace activists are going to have to accept the first lesson of politics: the art of the possible. No government is going to be able to deliver all we want in one fell swoop and the task after the election is going to be just as vital as the one before it. Our job is the mobilization of such an informed and concerned electorate so that any and every party will have to take seriously the disarmament issue at the next election. Careful parliamentary work over the last two years by CND and other groups has resulted in a much higher level of debate amongst politicians – who showed themselves so unprepared when they faced the 1983 election. Next time round nationalist slogans and drum-banging are not going to be nearly as effective.

The peace movement has also matured through the vigorous public debate of the last few years. We must move on from repeating the same types of activity – marches, of which people are perhaps tired – and challenge them with imaginative projects which will engage their talents in a direct and effective manner. Ideas take a long time to filter through, and there will be many who will only start to think for themselves once the daily abuse of a threatened establishment is no longer in the headlines. It is now that the real revolution – demanded by the unleashed power of the atom – can change our ways of thinking in a quieter, but more thoughtful and far-reaching conversion process going on at every pub, launderette, bus stop, school playground, M P's surgery and parish council.

The task is not just opposition to particular nuclear-weapon systems but, more positively, to spread the vision of a world, which is a perfectly possible world, where internationalism is more important than nationalism, where common security is more rational than individual security and where war, as a means of resolving conflict, is seen to be as barbaric as cannibalism is seen today as a means of augmenting one's diet.

But the time will come:

Nation shall not lift up a sword against nation, neither shall they learn war any more.

Micah iv, 3

Notes

1. *The Medical Effects of Nuclear War*, Report of the British Medical Association's Board of Science and Education, Chichester, John Wiley & Son, 1983.
2. *New Statesman*, 21 March 1986.
3. 'MI5's Official Secrets', film shown on Channel 4, March 1985.

4. *Education for Peace*, London, National Union of Teachers, 1984.
5. ibid.
6. Sr Joan Chittister, O S B: talk given to meeting of Pax Christi U S A's annual conference, 1985.
7. Reported in the *Guardian*, 25 May 1981.
8. *Safe and Sound – Disarmament and Development in the 1980s*, Clyde Sanger, London, Zed Press, 1982.
9. *Common Security: A Programme for Disarmament*, London, Pan Books, 1982.
10. *Defence Without the Bomb* (The Report of the Alternative Defence Commission) London, Taylor & Francis Ltd. 1983.
11. Joint Declaration of 22 May 1984.
12. See *The Times*, 15 August 1985.
13. *National Peace Council Annual Report 1981*, Sheila Oakes, London, National Peace Council, 1981.
14. *Unilateral Nuclear Disarmament Measures* – Report of the Secretary General of the United Nations, London, CND Publications, 1985.

Dan Smith: Afterword

The idea of de-alignment, explored and proposed in the essays in this book, is set against allegiance to one or other bloc. It differs from the idea of non-alignment in that the goal is not to stand aside from the blocs, but to end them. And while the perspective on that goal is necessarily long term, de-alignment must be understood not simply as an objective for the future but as a process which can be started now.

Before outlining policies which could begin the process, it is worth using the lens of de-alignment to look at arms control, especially in the wake of the October 1986 meeting between Messrs Gorbachov and Reagan in Reykjavik, which has made the arms-control situation more confused and confusing than it has ever been.

An ambitious package of major arms reductions was proposed by the Soviet side. Apparently negotiating from the hip, and alarming Western military circles as he did so, Reagan offered to discuss complete nuclear disarmament in a decade. Agreement was unattainable, ostensibly because the US administration remained as attached to Star Wars as the USSR was hostile to it. To have got so close and yet be so far from agreement was deeply disappointing. In the long run, the meeting's most important result may have been to offer a sight of the possibility of nuclear disarmament. Those discussions between the superpowers must have made the peace movements' goals look more practicable to more people. That slight taste of how things might be could well have whetted the public appetite.

However, the aftermath of Reykjavik showed the problems of relying on arms control. NATO generals argued that removing 'Intermediate Nuclear Forces' – cruise, Pershing II and SS-20 missiles – from Europe would leave NATO at a disadvantage, even though NATO has been claiming since 1979 that it wants such a deal. They sought to link agreement on INF with one on conventional and shorter-range nuclear forces, repeating the inaccurate argument that NATO is inferior in those categories. How bitterly we recall that NATO's deployment of cruise and Pershing II was always justified as a way of negotiating from strength to get rid of the SS-20s. The new linkage proposed by NATO circles is as wrong as the USSR's insistence on linking an INF agreement to Star Wars, where its case does not stand up in the way that it does in relation to strategic weapons.

NATO's post-Reykjavik gyrations reveal the flaws in 'negotiating from strength'. It cannot be argued that the USSR came to the talks because of US and NATO strength if it turns out that, in NATO's military judgement, the deal the West has been seeking will leave the USSR stronger. The reason for Gorbachov's proposals has nothing to do with the USA's insistence on negotiating from strength, and everything to do with his need to release industrial and technological resources to revitalize the Soviet economy. And if it were true that the only language the Soviet leadership understands is that of military strength, then it would always seek to negotiate from strength too. Obviously, as a mutually adopted negotiating tactic, the result would be the worst of all worlds – build-up, confrontation, hostility, and no arms reductions.

Even an arms-control process showing more progress than the grand zero of the past decade cannot substitute for the changes of policy and attitude needed to end the Cold War. Retaining the debilitating central assumptions about the permanence of the blocs, arms control is trapped in the problem it offers to solve. Any progress could be undermined and reversed by the persistence of bloc confrontation and its ambience of insecurity, tension and hostility – just as it was in the 1970s. Scepticism about the ability of arms control to deliver real arms cuts does not preclude a willingness to be pleasantly surprised. There is no question of scorning any real gains which might be produced. But arms control can never be enough without an accompanying process of de-alignment – an alternative approach which, starting from the reality of the blocs, offers a means of progressively changing and superseding that reality.

What then do we seek from governments in Western Europe?

At best, explicit rejection of the core tenets of Atlanticism – that is, of reliance on nuclear weapons, the dependent partnership with the USA, the permanence of Europe's division into military blocs.

At least, avoidance of actions which increase hostility and entrench confrontation, with overt opposition to such actions where possible, and even a modest contribution in the opposite direction.

Both the best and the least can be expressed as specific political and strategic initiatives. Some could be taken by individual states, others require cooperative action; some need no prior agreement with the USSR and its allies, others could or should be formalized in treaties. What follows is not a *programme* for gradual implementation, but a *menu*. Even the existing conservative governments in Western Europe can take the least ambitious steps, but governments with perspectives closer to the peace movements' will combine them with richer fare.

To begin with the least demanding steps:

● It is well within the capabilities of current Western European governments to make public criticisms of US policies – such as Star Wars, the refusal to conclude a comprehensive test-ban treaty, the pressure on Nicaragua and New Zealand – as vocal, for example, as criticisms of Soviet actions in Afghanistan.

● US pressure to expand NATO's range of operations should be met with a firm 'no', and it should be made clear that there will be no cooperation with US military adventures in the Mediterranean and Middle East.

These changes, restricted to the field of diplomacy, represent little more than saying in public what is widely said in private. Further refusals of US policy in which Western Europe is more centrally involved constitute a more demanding set of expectations:

● Technical cooperation in Star Wars research should be terminated and all talk of a European Defence Initiative laid to rest.

● Participation in the more aggressive postures and strategic doctrines introduced by the Reagan administration should be denied. This includes opposing the new naval strategy (with Britain refusing the use of Holy Loch or any other facility for submarines carrying cruise missiles) and rejecting the US Army's AirLand Battle Doctrine and its NATO derivatives.

● Public commitments against new nuclear and chemical weapons in Europe would force a reassessment of NATO's nuclear planning.

All this would slow the momentum of confrontation and start challenging NATO's predominant political and strategic assumptions. To underpin these changes as well as more ambitious ones, old strategic and political certainties need rethinking. There are two crucial issues:

● An alternative assessment of the military balance in Europe. American hawks grabbed the monopoly on this issue in the 1970s and their attitudes still shape official disinformation. Researchers have exposed its bogus basis, but it needs the authority of governments to convince most people that a non-alarmist assessment is entirely credible.

● Similarly, a different political assessment. It remains utterly incredible that the USSR wants to invade Western Europe for the sake of conquest. The threat of a westwards offensive is based on quite different problems. Yet both military planning and public justification for new weapons are still predicated on this myth, which prevents many people accepting the possibility of alternative policies.

Reassessing the basis of security policy needs to be accompanied by a new direction in foreign policy. In Britain, nostalgia for empire makes this need particularly profound. But there is a general requirement in Western Europe to free policy from the grip of the Cold War, especially in relation to the Third World. Some points stand out:

- Practical support and assistance for countries where the desire for an independent policy is squeezed by the superpowers.
- An increase in Official Development Assistance.
- A reconsideration of the debt problem, including unhitching the terms of borrowing from the fluctuations in exchange and interest rates.

Similarly, we need constructive policies towards the USSR and Eastern Europe, creating more economic, political and cultural ties across the divide. Policies for a new detente include:

- Re-invigorating the 'Helsinki process', not as an arena for rhetorical confrontation, but as a framework for more far-reaching agreements on cultural and political openness.
- Bilateral agreements, including ones on common security and demilitarization, such as those reached between East Germany and the West German SPD on nuclear- and chemical-weapon-free zones.

The most ambitious steps break directly with the core components of the Atlanticist consensus:
- Re-organizing the NATO hierarchy to deny the USA its dominant voice.
- Withdrawal from nuclear roles.
- Expulsion of US nuclear bases. This can be expressed as a 'sub-menu', since there are different kinds of nuclear base:
  bases where nuclear weapons are stored;
  bases into which nuclear weapons could be flown at short notice;
  bases from which nuclear-capable weapons systems operate;

bases which are part of the USA's world-wide nuclear network.

- Non-provocative, non-nuclear defence policies.
- Expulsion of all US bases. The problem of doing this in the Federal Republic of Germany where, formally, American (like British and French) forces are still occupation forces, would have to be addressed by recognizing that this anachronistic limit on the Federal Republic's sovereignty must be lifted.

Even the most modest of these actions would challenge the momentum of the Cold War. Taken together they mean a major shift not just in the policy but in the philosophy of security in Western Europe. Any government adopting any part of this approach will face intense pressure to desist. That is one reason why the more governments that do it the better. But it is entirely improbable that such policies will be adopted simultaneously throughout the European NATO states. And while it is the job of peace movements to present an ambitious prospectus, to demand not the least but the best, it is also part of the task to relate our goals to the immediate political situation of each country.

No Western European political party with a real chance of forming an administration has a programme which fully meets the vision of the peace movements. The SPD in West Germany (where an election will have been held by the time this book is published) and the Labour Party in Britain (where one is in the offing) have taken on parts of it, but neither has properly absorbed the need to surmount the mentality of bloc confrontation. The Labour Party's proposals on nuclear disarmament are radical, but it is otherwise playing the role of loyal NATO member, apparently accepting the alliance's basic assumptions.

Even so, in Britain, the best chance of implementing significant items on the agenda of de-alignment is the election of a Labour government. The danger and mean-spiritedness of Conservative policy were illustrated again when Mrs Thatcher scuttled to Washington after the Reykjavik meeting to warn the President against his unsettling ideas about nuclear disarmament and insist on Britain's right to the illusory status symbol of Trident. The SDP/Liberal Alliance has driven itself into a cul-de-sac, hankering for bargain-basement nuclear weapons and chasing the hare of Franco-British nuclear cooperation, tempted in some quarters by the notion of a European mini-superpower. The idea that 'Europe' consists of the EEC has always been wrong, and now it's becoming dangerous, striking against the concept of common security to which Dr Owen once gave his name, but which in practice he can't support because of his nuclear fixation.

Labour's election, however, is not enough, and not just because of reservations about its policies. Support for nuclear disarmament and aspects of de-alignment extends beyond party boundaries. Electing MPs of other parties with commitments to these policies – personal or party commitments or, preferably, both – is as important. Moreover, a narrow focus on a Labour win risks despair if it doesn't happen. Whatever our impatience, however sharply we perceive the urgency of a new approach to security, we should not underestimate the scale of the task we have set ourselves of shaping a political atmosphere in which nuclear disarmament commands a clear majority in public opinion. However the parties fare electorally, that task will remain. Politics does not stop with an election, whatever its outcome.

These considerations define a complex peace-movement agenda requiring much energy, imagination and sensitivity. It remains crucial to mobilize resistance to the arms race and Cold War, to develop new ideas and to gain widespread public support for them. Yet the peace movements' role is perhaps even more important when it comes to implementing new policies.

When governments are elected on platforms which include items from the agenda of de-alignment, the movements' responsibilities will become even more onerous. Our approach generates deep hostility from those still loyal to an increasingly impoverished orthodoxy. The deployment of cruise and Pershing I I missiles and the pressure on the Greek government not to expel nuclear bases revealed the sort of efforts which will be made to frustrate implementation of new policies. Peace movements have the potential to counter that pressure on the basis of a public appeal which reaches further than any party's electoral base. This calls for a discriminating mixture of criticism as necessary and encouragement as appropriate, while continuing the work of informing, changing and mobilizing public opinion. The international networks developed by the movements will have an essential role in creating an international counterweight to efforts to orchestrate pressure within NATO on any government stepping out of line.

For this to happen, peace movements will need great sensitivity and a renewed degree of closeness. It will also be essential that a government moving some way along the path of disarmament and de-alignment, however it presents its policies, is scrupulously open about the forms of pressure it is facing and retains creative links with the movements whose ideas provide much of its inspiration.

Seven years after their initial upsurge, the peace movements of the 1980s have a full agenda and a long road to travel. We shall need all the remarkable strength and creativity they have sustained for so long already. Nobody ever said it would be easy. But at least the signposts are clearly marked and the journey has begun.

November 1986

Notes on Contributors

APRIL CARTER has been involved in the nuclear-disarmament movement since 1958. She has taught politics at the University of Lancaster, with the Open University and, from 1976 to 1984, at Somerville College, Oxford. She is now a freelance peace researcher, and her main commitment in recent years has been to the Alternative Defence Commission.

JIRI DIENSTBIER lives in Czechoslovakia and was a well-known radio commentator during the 'Prague Spring' in 1968. In January 1979 he became a spokesperson for the Charter 77 human rights movement and, shortly afterwards, was sentenced to three years imprisonment on political charges. In 1985 he served as a spokesperson for Charter 77 for a second time.

MARY KALDOR is a Fellow of the Transnational Institute in Amsterdam and a Senior Fellow of the Science Policy Research Unit at Sussex University. She is editor of *END Journal*. Her publications include *The Disintegrating West* (1978) and *The Baroque Arsenal* (1982).

BRUCE KENT is known nationally and internationally as the leading spokesperson of the Campaign for Nuclear Disarmament. One time administrator of Catholic schools, university chaplain and parish priest, he was General Secretary of CND from 1980 to 1985, and is now a vice-chair. He is ex-chair of War on Want and is President of the International Peace Bureau.

DAN SMITH is a researcher and writer, Fellow of the Transnational Institute in Amsterdam, vice-chairperson of CND and a former chairperson of END. He was co-editor of *Protest and Survive* (1980) and co-author of *The War Atlas* (1983).

KATE SOPER is a philosopher and writer. She teaches part-time at the Polytechnic of North London and is author of *On Human Needs*

(1981) and *Humanism and Anti-Humanism* (1986). She is chairperson of END.

JONATHAN STEELE is Chief Foreign Correspondent of the *Guardian*. He has reported extensively from the Soviet Union, the USA, and various parts of the Third World. His books include *The South African Connection: Western Investment in Apartheid* and *The Limits of Soviet Power* (1985).

E. P. THOMPSON is a historian and writer. He is a vice-president of CND and an active member of END, and has visited the USA, Canada and many European countries for the peace movement. His recent books on these questions include *The Heavy Dancers* and *Double Exposure* (1985), and (co-edited with Ben Thompson) *Star Wars* (1985).

ZDENA TOMIN is a playwright and novelist, now living in London. Born during the German occupation of Czechoslovakia in 1941, she graduated in philosophy at Charles University in Prague a month before the Soviet invasion in 1968. In 1979 and 1980 she was one of the spokespersons for Charter 77. In 1981 the Czech authorities withdrew her citizenship while she was visiting England. Her novel, *Stalin's Shoe* was published in 1985.

CAESAR VOÛTE is a Dutchman who now lives and works in London. He has been active with local CND groups in East Anglia, and was for two years convenor of END's Hungary working group.